THE GOSPEL TRUTH

AN EXPLORATION OF THE GOSPEL OF PAUL

SCOTT FORBES

The Gospel Truth: An Exploration of the Gospel of Paul

Published by Forbescraft Press
Neosho, MO 64850

LCCN 2011941502

ISBN 978-0-61-555769-4

Printed in the United States of America

For two brides –

Susan, my patient wife and beloved friend.
And the Bride of Christ,
whom I pray will once again
abandon the wisdom of the world
for the power of God

Acknowledgements

I wish to thank the following for making this work possible:

First of all I thank my Heavenly Father, without whom none of this would be comprehensible, and Jesus Christ who died that I might be pardoned and lives that I might live with Him, and the Holy Spirit who searches the deep things of God and reveals them to men. My only hope is that these words honor You.

Susan, my wife, for editing my scribbles. Thanks for the honesty and kindness with which you make order out of chaos!

To a number of friends who encourage me in my lunacy; Joel Anthes, Robert Crumb, Brian Spade, Russell and Jennifer Duncan, Greg Franklin, Doctor Jean Hobbs and (well, yeah) my beloved and greatly missed Ms. Leota Hill. I look forward to seeing you again, 'honey'.

I thank my dad for praying for me without ceasing when I was young and saw no need for God. Without those prayers and the prayers of many others, I would not be writing this today.

If I have forgotten anyone, please forgive me. The influences on my life have been too many to mention; you are all important to me. Thank you.

CONTENTS

INTRODUCTION 9

ORIGIN AND POWER 15

PREACHING 51

SEND THE LIGHT! 71

THROWING THE BOOK 83

HOW SWEET THE SOUND 107

THE COMFORTER 125

REVISITING LAW: THE POWER OF SIN 139

THE THRESHOLD 153

AFTERWORD 165

REFERENCES AND RESOURCES 169

INTRODUCTION

This is not the original introduction to this book. In fact, as it turns out, this is not the original book at all. It is something that has evolved from the original concept of a book which would both outline evangelism strategies and the reasons for those strategies. You can, in places, still see vestiges of the original purpose. But for the most part it is a horse of a different color than first envisioned.

As I thought about re-writing this introduction, my mind kept returning to something unspiritual and yet very appropriate to what I feel the book has become. Any of you that watched the Seinfeld television series may remember an episode where George discovered that if he did the opposite of what came instinctually to him, things worked out much better in his life. The study I did in the preparation of this book has shown me that the gospel and scripture in general is much like that. If we try to interpret it based on our human instincts we will get it wrong ninety-nine percent of the time. Almost invariably, scripture makes more sense if we approach it one-hundred and eighty degrees out of our natural thought patterns. This is what Paul is urging the church at Corinth to do in the scripture that opens this introduction (2 Corinthians 10:5).

This is not to say that scripture is insulting to our intelligence. Quite frankly, I have found my own intellect to be an insult to scripture. The truths of The Bible are much deeper and richer than I could ever have imagined and far more strange and wonderful. Common sense, though a wonderful thing in its own right, can be a detriment to us when we approach scripture.

My prayer is that God will open the eyes of your heart to understand the deep mystery of what we call the gospel. I pray that you will realize that all of Christian existence flows from the good news of what God has done for us through Jesus Christ. I will echo the prayer of Paul for the church at Ephesus: "I pray that you, being rooted and established in love, may have power, together with all the saints, to grasp how wide and long and high and deep is the love of Christ, and to know this love that surpasses knowledge—that you may be filled to the measure of all the fullness of God."[1]

This book is not a challenge to *do* anything. We already have enough 'how-to' books and sermons in our lives. My purpose is

[1] EPHESIANS 3:17-19

to show you that the kingdom of God has far less to do with principled living than it does the power of God; less 'doing' and more 'being'. I think that we, in the west, have long ago abandoned the power that was evident in the early church because we can't wrap our heads around it. We cannot build programs around mysteries that cannot be taught except through the Holy Spirit, and we don't know how to do 'Christian' without programs.

I hope to help you take the ancient gospel out of the closet of your mind and look at it with new eyes. It may have been many years since you believed it. Perhaps it long ago became to you just one of many aspects Christian life; the haunt of evangelists. Or perhaps you think of it merely as the doorway to Christian understanding. It may have been ten, twenty, or fifty years since you passed through that 'door', and now you seldom even consider it. I am here to remind you, perhaps to show you for the first time, that the gospel is not simply a doorway but the very ground upon which, if we belong to Christ, we all stand.

Though few recognize it, there is perhaps no area of Christian doctrine that has been more neglected, twisted and diluted than the gospel itself. Scripture is definitely not mute on the subject, but for whatever reason we have chosen to ignore most of what is revealed to us regarding the message of reconciliation which God has given us. Our modern gospel is incoherent; it makes no sense to the average person – even the average

Christian. When Luke writes of Paul's preaching throughout the Book of Acts, he uses terms like 'reasoned', 'taught' and 'persuaded'. Paul's message was therefore reasonable, teachable, and persuasive, unlike much of today's 'gospel' message.

The Christian faith is by no means a blind faith. The gospel, as revealed throughout The Bible, is intellectually satisfying. Our God is not a God of disorder, so the gospel he gave is a cohesive, ordered, powerful kind of knowledge. The fact that people must hear the gospel before they can place their faith in Christ shows that it must be a special kind of knowledge which leads people to the savior, not a call to blind, unreasoned faith. The biblical gospel engages the mind and the conscience, as well as the emotions.

If you can grasp what The Bible has to say regarding the gospel in these pages, you will undoubtedly begin to see it richly illustrated throughout all of scripture. The gospel is, in fact, the central theme of The Bible and much of The Bible can only be understood once a complete understanding of the gospel has come. The gospel was the driving force behind the apostles, the reason for their existence and writings, and the purpose for the law and the prophets. This message is the only true theme of Christianity; the gateway to a relationship with the living God. The gospel of scripture is the narrow door, but it is so much more than that. The scriptural gospel is to be the standard of Christian living; the motivation behind our lives – the narrow path as well. Paul said, "Whatever happens, conduct yourselves in a manner worthy of the gospel of Christ."[2] In removing most of the divinely revealed truth of the gospel, we have inadvertently removed the powerful basis for the Christian life, all the while wondering why the church has become impotent!

Perhaps when you are finished with the book you will come to understand why Paul was not ashamed of the gospel. Not that my words are any great illumination of it, but if you can get the tiniest taste of the greatness of the gospel message, I know your appetite will grow. May you then find that you are more willing to share it, as each of us knows that we should, without the guilt trip. Share it for the sole reason it is so exceedingly excellent and liberating. If you get to that point, solid resources on how to share it have been written by Ray Comfort and Mark Cahill and I would suggest that you consult their works if you want to learn solid biblical methods of evangelism. Please refer to the References and Resources section at the end of the book for more information.

Now, let us explore the mystery of God.

[2] PHILIPPIANS 1:27

ORIGIN AND POWER

I WANT YOU TO KNOW, BROTHERS, THAT THE GOSPEL I PREACHED IS NOT SOMETHING THAT MAN MADE UP. I DID NOT RECEIVE IT FROM ANY MAN, NOR WAS I TAUGHT IT; RATHER, I RECEIVED IT BY REVELATION FROM JESUS CHRIST.

GALATIANS 1:11-12

The noonday sun shown hot over the dry land. So hot you could taste the dust from the road. It had been a long day already, and the men were road-weary. Despite their weariness, they were excited to be nearing their destination.

They spoke as they travelled of beds and food and drink that awaited them in Damascus, of all that was happening throughout Judea, and of the purpose of their mission. They took no little pride in having been allowed this assignment – a great service to God. The leader of the group held on his person a letter from the high priest which gave them permission to arrest anyone in the city found to belong to a Nazarene sect which called themselves 'The Way'. These sectarians were threatening the status quo in Jerusalem and had to be stopped. This leader's name was Saul, of the city of Tarsus. He was a Pharisee of Pharisees, an up-and-comer in his faith. He was full of zeal for God and a desire to stop anyone or anything that threatened the Jewish religious system.

The rooftops of Damascus appeared in the distance, shimmering over the road in the heat. The pace now quickened. There was laughter among the group. Then silence.

A blinding white light suddenly enveloped the men. Saul dropped to the ground, while the others stood stunned, jaws dropping open. There was a sound like thunder. And in the thunder, Saul alone heard a voice. The voice of Jesus Christ. He received a new assignment- "Rise and go into the city, and you will be told what you are to do".[1]

Blinded by the light which had flashed around him, Saul was helpless and had to be led by his companions into the city. They led him to the house of Judas on Straight Street. And there he waited in utter blindness, physically and spiritually. What happened during those hours of darkness is somewhat of a mystery; a mystery that redirected Saul's life and the course of history.

The Gospel I Preached

We know of several incidents that occurred during this time. In Acts chapter nine we find that the Lord told Ananias, a believer in Jesus Christ, to pray for Saul so that he might receive

---

[1] ACTS 9:6

his sight back. He also told him that Saul, soon to be known as Paul, "is my chosen instrument to carry my name before the Gentiles and their kings and before the people of Israel."[2] Ananias told Paul, "The God of our fathers has chosen you to know his will and to see the Righteous One and to hear words from his mouth. You will be his witness to all men of what you have seen and heard."[3]

What was it that Paul heard from the Righteous One in Damascus? We don't fully know, but the change in his life and the power of his preaching after this time is evidence that it was a message. A message of reconciliation between God and man. A message of exceedingly good news. The gospel truth.

Acts 9:20 tells us that after being baptized Paul "At once began to preach in the synagogues that Jesus is the Son of God", strong evidence that he had heard, understood and placed confidence in the message he had received.

Fourteen years after this gospel revelation, he went to Jerusalem to consult with the church leaders in Judea. According to Galatians 2, James, Peter and John "saw that I had been entrusted with the gospel to the uncircumcised, just as Peter had been entrusted with the gospel to the circumcised (for he who worked through Peter for his apostolic ministry to the circumcised worked also through me for mine to the

---

[2] ACTS 8:15
[3] ACTS 22:14

Gentiles)..."[4]

So God had established, through Paul, a specific gospel message to the Gentiles, and this message was given to him by direct revelation from the Lord (see Galatians 1:11-12 in the opening of this chapter). Take a moment to think about that. He never guessed what the gospel message should be. He never had to think it over and try to make sense of it and boil it down into something that he could market to others. He just received it from God, and then he preached it.

Throughout the New Testament, Paul preached this powerful message. With it, he and a handful of other first-century evangelists established the church throughout the known world. Since the dynamic message that they preached was given by the direct revelation of God, it explains the explosive influence of the first century church. They were sharing what they had received directly from God, which brought the power of God to the unbelieving world around them.

A Flash of Light

Could the power of Paul's preaching be traced to his experience on the road to Damascus? It was an encounter that changed his life. In the space of a few paragraphs in the Book of Acts, Paul goes from being the hateful persecutor of the church

[4] GALATIANS 2:7-8 (ESV)

to becoming one of its most outspoken and powerful leaders.

But though it appears often in his testimony, and is mentioned occasionally in his epistles, he never bragged about it. In referring to this experience Paul said, "and last of all he appeared to me also, as to one abnormally born."[5] He downplays this experience rather than using it to provide weight to his preaching, as if to intentionally keep people from thinking he was extraordinary because of it.

Any one of us who has placed our faith in Jesus Christ as our savior has had a supernatural encounter with God. We have each had our own Damascus Road experience. In fact, since we have never seen the Lord nor heard his voice, is it not more marvelous that we believe? Jesus said to the disciples, "Because you have seen me, you have believed; blessed are those who have not seen and yet have believed."[6] Never think that your own salvation experience is any less miraculous than that of any other. Every salvation is a miracle, without exception.

An Unchanging Message

What made Paul truly remarkable was not his preaching ability or his supernatural experience, but his obedience. God gave him a message and 'at once' he began to preach that message without question. There is no indication that he ever

---

[5] 1 CORINTHIANS 5:8
[6] JOHN 20:29

doubted the message which was given him, and he never wavered from it. He states that he never consulted any man, nor did he immediately go to see the other apostles[7] before he launched into the work to which he had been called. The fact that he set about preaching 'at once' speaks to his confidence in the power of that message and of God. There was no development time, no need to polish it or hone it, no need to add to it, no opinion polls or felt needs surveys taken; just the immediate, obedient desire to preach.

Twenty plus years after his Damascus Road experience, Paul, speaking of the gospel he had preached to the Corinthians, wrote:

"Now, brothers and sisters, I want to remind you of the gospel I preached to you, which you received and on which you have taken your stand… For what I received I passed on to you as of first importance: that Christ died for our sins according to the Scriptures, that he was buried, that he was raised on the third day according to the Scriptures…"[8]

He had been faithful to the message throughout the years and continued to affirm it. What he received, he continued to pass on throughout his lifetime without alteration.

Paul was passionate about this message. He lived to preach

---

[7] GALATIANS 1:15-17
[8] 1 CORINTHIANS 15:1-3

it. He died for preaching it. He knew it forward, backward and inside out. No matter where he found himself or who he found himself with, he preached it boldly. And he preached it with accuracy. He understood that God had entrusted him with secrets[9] which he must reveal faithfully.

If we want to know how strongly Paul felt about accurate preaching, we need look no further than Galatians 1:8. Here he says,

> "But even if we or an angel from heaven should preach a gospel other than the one we preached to you, let him be eternally condemned!"

He calls for his own condemnation should he ever preach another gospel. Not only would Paul not tolerate the perversion of the gospel by others, he took steps to insure that he would not be welcomed by the church if he ever came preaching a different message. Clearly he trusted the message more than he trusted himself. He guarded it jealously.

The Power of God

Once we understand the origin of the gospel, we can understand the source of its power. Just as it originates with God, it also draws its power from God. One of the greatest victories that Satan could ever have would be to convince the

---

[9] 1 CORINTHIANS 4:1

church that the message of the cross alone is not powerful enough to save. If he could trick us into re-writing the gospel, packaging it as something that appeals to the carnal mind; if he could make us think that solely preaching the scriptural gospel without endless follow-up work was fruitless (or even cruelty) it would mean the death of evangelism. If he could get us to deny the fact that the gospel is the very power of God for salvation, he could so slow the advance of the gospel as to bring it to a near standstill. Or better yet, he could get us to create an army of people who are convinced by an 'almost' gospel that they are saved when they were not. Unfortunately, he has been successful in getting us to believe and do all of this, largely unaware of his influence.

Paul stated his view of the gospel in Romans 1:16:

"I am not ashamed of the gospel, because it is the power of God for the salvation of everyone who believes: first for the Jew, then for the Gentile."

It is no wonder then that his supreme confidence in the gospel (which at times could almost be mistaken for arrogance) appears throughout all of his epistles with remarkable clarity. In contrast to our modern 'anything goes' mentality toward evangelism, Paul understood that there was only one gospel. He referred to it as 'my gospel' three times and 'our gospel' four more times in the New Testament. It was a very specific, powerful and concise message which led men to an understanding of the grace of God.

When I ask Christians what it means to be saved, I am often surprised at the answers I get. Most cannot explain in scriptural terms what grace is or how it works. Many cannot even guess at the reason why God saves us, other than to say that He loves *us* and wants the best for *us*. By contrast, when we read the epistles of Paul, it is hard to find a chapter that does not in some way relate back to a deep understanding of grace that governed his faith, life and work. He focused his energies on preaching and living out the gospel as an active, all-consuming passion, not merely a better lifestyle. It was the rock upon which his life and ministry were built, a gift of deep and secret knowledge which God had graciously made known to him. Though it belonged to God, it had been given to him and he spent himself giving it to others.

Do you own the gospel in that sense? Have you made it your most cherished possession? Is the message you think of as the gospel something that creates deep passion in you? We think of the things that we own very differently from things that we don't. If you rent a car, do you wash it, change the oil, drive it carefully and take it around to show all your family and friends? No, it's just a rental. You may exercise caution with it because you know you have to pay for any damage to it, but you don't passionately enjoy it and share it. When we own something, we cherish it, maintain it, know it, enjoy it, feel comfortable using it and even boast about it. And we are free to give away only that which we truly own. Is that how you feel about the gospel or do you treat it like it's something that belongs to someone else? Hopefully at some point you can know it and appreciate it enough to think of it as 'my gospel', as did Paul.

Treasure in Clay Jars

When we discount the inherent power of the gospel itself, we can begin thinking that it requires a special ability to preach it. We might imagine that the spread of the gospel evident in the Book of Acts was made possible by the unique abilities of the early disciples. As we read the writings of Paul we see that he lived and breathed faith. We imagine him as a person of powerful presence because of his writings. But was that so? Scripture shows that Paul, to some of his hearers, did not have much presence at all. To the Corinthians Paul wrote of himself, "Some say, 'His letters are weighty and forceful, but in person he is unimpressive and his speaking amounts to nothing.'"[10] Though Paul made it clear that those with such a view were merely looking on the surface of things and ignoring the power beneath[11], to some his personal presence was apparently underwhelming. This should not be surprising in a man who

[10] 2 CORINTHIANS 10:10
[11] 2 CORINTHIANS 10:7

understood that the Lord's power is made perfect in weakness[12]. It follows then that Paul did not place his confidence in his ability as a preacher, but in God and the message he had to deliver; a message that was powerful despite the weakness of the one delivering it.

There is other evidence that Paul relied completely on the power of the message and the Holy Spirit when he preached. Witness 1 Corinthians 2:1-5:

"When I came to you, brothers, I did not come with eloquence or superior wisdom as I proclaimed to you the testimony about God. For I resolved to know nothing while I was with you except Jesus Christ and him crucified. I came to you in weakness and fear, and with much trembling. My message and my preaching were not with wise and persuasive words, but with a demonstration of the Spirit's power, so that your faith might not rest on men's wisdom, but on God's power."

Are these the words of a man who trusted in his ability as a preacher? If you have ever preached the gospel, you can certainly relate to Paul's fear and trembling as he preached to the Corinthians. The biblical gospel is unbending and ruthlessly intolerant of sin; it can be frightening to preach. If you exhibit these symptoms while sharing the gospel message, you are in good company.

[12] 2 CORINTHIANS 12:9

Here is the difference between Paul's preaching and the modern gospel: despite his fears, he did not resort to reliance on wise and persuasive words or emotional pleas to make his message more palatable. Relying on a demonstration of the Spirit's power, he clearly proclaimed the 'testimony about God'. The power was in that testimony and scripture makes it clear that Paul understood this.

Paul spoke of the glory of the gospel of Christ as a treasure, noting that "we have this treasure in jars of clay to show that this all-surpassing power is from God and not from us."[13] God intentionally used (and uses) weak vessels from which to pour forth this treasure so that it may be clearly seen that the power is His alone. This is not to say that He will not use those with dynamic presence for this task; we know that He has and does use men of great intellect and speaking ability in the ministry of the gospel. It is to say that God uses humble men, men who are aware of their weakness and frailty and who have emptied themselves so that they might carry this great treasure.

No one is competent in themselves to be a gospel preacher. God does not expect us to be competent but to put our confidence in the message He has given us to preach. Paul wrote to the Corinthians,

"Not that we are competent in ourselves to claim anything for ourselves, but our competence comes from

---

[13] 2 CORINTHIANS 4:7

God. He has made us competent as ministers of a new covenant—not of the letter but of the Spirit; for the letter kills, but the Spirit gives life."[14]

There was no doubt in Paul's mind that his ability as a minister of the life-giving gospel came from God alone.

Wonderworking Power

Many in the church today view stranger evangelism as destructive, saying that sharing the gospel with someone the evangelist is unlikely to see again is merely selling 'fire insurance'. In other words, they think personal evangelism without personal follow-up leads people to an 'I-got-my-ticket-to-heaven' mentality, and it can if we use a message other than that which God has given us. But when, through the scriptural gospel, someone recognizes their absolute dependence on God for His mercy, it makes sense that they will want to live to please Him. We need merely trust in the power of the message to bring them to Christ, and the power of the Holy Spirit to keep them there, which The Bible clearly teaches.

In Acts 8, we find the story of Phillip and the Ethiopian eunuch. Following the leading of the Spirit, Phillip preached from the scriptures to an Ethiopian government official on the road leaving Samaria. The preaching must have hit the mark, for when they came to water, the man asked Phillip to baptize

[14] 2 CORINTHIANS 3:5-6

him. Scripture relates that "when they came up out of the water, the Spirit of the Lord suddenly took Philip away, and the eunuch did not see him again, but went on his way rejoicing."[15] It is interesting to note that in his joy at understanding the gospel, the Ethiopian doesn't seem to even question Phillip's disappearance! But more importantly, consider the fact that God left this man with no follow-up other than the scriptures he had been reading when he met Phillip. God is confident in His ability to save. Are we?

The biblical gospel is powerful enough to save regardless of the motivation of the one preaching it. It's hard to believe that anyone would preach the gospel out of impure motives, but observe Paul's response as he records this very thing happening in Philippians chapter 1:

"It is true that some preach Christ out of envy and rivalry, but others out of goodwill. The latter do so in love, knowing that I am put here for the defense of the gospel. The former preach Christ out of selfish ambition, not sincerely, supposing that they can stir up trouble for me while I am in chains. But what does it matter? The important thing is that in every way, whether from false motives or true, Christ is preached. And because of this I rejoice."[16]

---

[15] ACTS 8:39
[16] PHILIPPIANS 1:15-18

Paul rejoices that Christ is preached. Can you be any more confident of a message than to *not care what the motive is in preaching it?* He understands that the power of God is in the message and not the messenger and so it makes little difference to him why the gospel is preached, so long as it is preached.

If we could let that sink in, it would have dynamic impact on our view of evangelism. I am not in any way advocating preaching the gospel out of spite, but what of the days when we don't feel like witnessing? Has God ever dropped a perfect opportunity in your lap and you passed it up because you didn't feel up to the task? Wouldn't it make some difference to know that the power of God, which is integral in the biblical gospel, does the work regardless of how you feel or how poorly you speak? If we lack confidence as evangelists, it should be self-confidence. If we lack confidence in our message, the problem is that we are preaching the wrong message. We can and must have complete confidence in God and *His* gospel if we are to preach faithfully.

The work of salvation is the work of the Holy Spirit. It is supernatural - beyond the realm of worldly understanding. Therefore, it makes sense that the message by which we introduce people to Christ must be supernaturally powerful to save. God, the author and finisher of our faith, has provided us with just such a message. If we began working alongside the Holy Spirit speaking the very message that He delivered to the early church, could we possibly see three or five thousand solidly saved in a day? If those whom God has called respond to practically any 'gospel' message, how much greater would the response be to the God-given message of reconciliation?

Two Kinds of Wisdom

The gospel is a special kind of message. We may be able to bring someone to intellectually acknowledge God using apologetics, and we may be able to bring someone to emotional assent using personal testimony and dramatic appeals, but we can never bring them to God by these methods alone. Only the gospel can bring people to a place where they begin to understand something which can never be taught; the mind of God.

Godly wisdom is completely foreign to the world. They know it neither by experience nor by education; it is God given. When we present the gospel, we are presenting an idea that the human mind will never grasp unless God brings enlightenment. We are attempting to break down the wall of worldly wisdom so that people can get a glimpse of Godly wisdom, hoping that this brings an appetite for the things of God.

We have the idea that the message we preach must have worldly appeal – it must be attractive to sinners. As a result, we have 'patched it up', hiding what we perceive to be the ugly truths and foolishness that it contains. In so doing we have, in the wisdom of the world, abandoned Godly wisdom in the preaching of the gospel. There is no scriptural evidence that Paul ever changed his message to suit anyone. In actuality, he warned of the difference between worldly wisdom and Godly wisdom as it relates to the gospel. He stated that we should preach "not with words of human wisdom, lest the cross of Christ be emptied of its power".[17] If we preach a gospel of human wisdom, we can literally make the powerful message of the cross ineffective.

What is worse is that we can derail the lives of those to whom we preach, leading them into false hope. Paul was keenly aware of the responsibility that had been given him along with the gospel revelation. He knew that the spiritual livelihood of his hearers depended on his accurate preaching. He said to the Corinthians that he preached "with a demonstration of the Spirit's power, so that your faith might not rest on men's wisdom, but on God's power."[18] In other words, when we preach the wisdom of men, people who respond may actually put their hope in our 'wisdom', believing that it is God's wisdom. When that wisdom turns out to be faulty, they will most likely blame God and their hearts will be hardened to any further gospel teaching.

By putting together clever words and arguments to try and

[17] 1 CORINTHIANS 1:17
[18] 1 CORINTHIANS 2:5

appeal to human understanding and lure people to Christ with human wisdom, we are quenching the Spirit. The scriptural gospel will always illicit some reaction from those who hear it. Paul said of the Thessalonians,

> "For we know, brothers loved by God, that he has chosen you, because our gospel came to you not simply with words, but also with power, with the Holy Spirit and with deep conviction."[19]

To Paul, it was apparent that the Thessalonians had believed the gospel; he saw the outworking of God's power in their reaction to it. He was not looking for 'decisions', he was looking for the evidence of God working in the lives of his hearers. We must, with Paul, understand that "the kingdom of God is not a matter of talk but of power."[20] If we preach anything short of a biblical gospel it is merely talk; devoid or deprived of power. If the experience of the last 100 years is any indication, this kind of talk tends to result in faith of a similar nature; all talk and no power.

The countenance of someone under the conviction of the Holy Spirit will change. There may be tears or there may be anger, but the power of God in the biblical gospel message will affect everyone you preach to in one way or another. The gospel, being intolerant of sin, is offensive to the carnal mind. If

---

[19] 1 THESSALONIANS 1:4-5
[20] 1 CORINTHIANS 4:20

you can preach without any visible reaction, it is a serious indication that you are not preaching the right gospel. John Wesley said, "If the gospel is preached well, sinners should be angry or convicted of sin, righteousness, and judgment to come." And so they should.

Gospel Relevance

In the western world, the church has been fighting a losing battle against moral relativism; the belief that there is no absolute truth. We claim to have absolute truth as revealed in the Word of God, yet we frequently adapt or ignore that truth to meet our needs or the perceived needs of others. This is true of the modern gospel message; we have adopted an evangelism strategy that weighs whether or not certain truths of the gospel apply to the individual to whom we are preaching. We tailor our message to meet the perceived needs of the listener. We preach a relativistic gospel.

Some might argue that we really don't have a pattern for the gospel message (the absolute gospel, if you will) and if that were true, then this kind of experimental approach to preaching might be reasonable. But if The Bible indicates that the gospel is a specific message (as we have said before and shall see as we continue) which was given by direct revelation from God, would that not be considered the 'true' gospel? And if we have the 'true' gospel, would that not make all other gospels 'false'?

There are many religions that teach a way to heaven, but they differ enough that they cannot all be true. They are either all false, or one is true and all others false, but they cannot all be true. All of scripture, including the scripturally revealed gospel, can be thought of the same way. If there really is a biblical gospel, that message alone can be preached as truth; all others become false gospels.

The relativistic gospel view holds that we need to discover people's worldview or felt needs so we can make our message relevant to their situation. I can find no scriptural evidence that Paul modified his gospel in this way, apparently because he understood that the gospel addressed the need for righteousness before God, which is not changed by a person's situation. Regardless of worldview or felt needs, all have sinned and fallen short of the glory of God[21] and need to hear the gospel call to repentance.

I can imagine some might object from 2 Corinthians 9:20-23, "But Paul became all things to all men so that by all possible means he might save some. Doesn't that mean that he tailored his message to his hearers?" On the contrary, he tailored himself to his hearers. Here is the text:

> "To the Jews I became like a Jew, to win the Jews. To those under the law I became like one under the law (though I myself am not under the law), so as to win those

---

[21] ROMANS 3:23

under the law. To those not having the law I became like one not having the law (though I am not free from God's law but am under Christ's law), so as to win those not having the law. To the weak I became weak, to win the weak. I have become all things to all men so that by all possible means I might save some. *I do all this for the sake of the gospel, that I may share in its blessings."*

Since the power lies within the message and not the messenger, it is perfectly allowable for us to tailor *ourselves* to suit our hearers (so long as we don't compromise our witness). We may imitate the customs of those around us, creating a comfortable environment in which to share our message. Paul became like his hearers so as to put them at ease and was careful not to offend their customs and sensibilities, which in turn provided him opportunity to speak into their lives. But if we take a close look at verse 23 we realize that the gospel stands apart from this tailoring. Paul says, "I do all this for the *sake of the gospel...*" This indicates that his habit of ingratiating himself to others was means to the end of preaching the gospel, not that he preached an ingratiating gospel message. His gospel remained intact regardless of any attempts he made to endear himself to his audience, and despite the fact that he preached the gospel message to people with a wide range of beliefs and lifestyles.

We know he preached to both Jews and Greeks, two very

diverse people groups with differing 'worldviews':

> "Jews demand miraculous signs and Greeks look for
> wisdom, but we preach Christ crucified: a stumbling
> block to Jews and foolishness to Gentiles, but to those
> whom God has called, both Jews and Greeks, Christ the
> power of God and the wisdom of God."[22]

He acknowledges that each of these people groups react to his
message in very different ways. Note, however, that he is not
concerned with what his audience is 'demanding' or 'looking
for'. He remains true to his message because he knows that
those whom God is calling will recognize the power of God in
the message *regardless* of their beliefs and customs. The called
ones will accept this wisdom that comes from God.

The Calling of God

The importance of this 'calling' of God cannot be overstated.
If we fail to understand that those who will believe have been
called of God it can lead to nothing but frustration in our
evangelical efforts. Our only obligation is to preach accurately –
we are not responsible for results.

In the first chapter of Ephesians, Paul identifies four essential
elements of salvation; God's calling, hearing the truth, believing,
and the marking of the Holy Spirit:

[22] 1 CORINTHIANS 1:22-25

"In him [Christ] we were also chosen, having been predestined according to the plan of him who works out everything in conformity to the purpose of his will... And you also were included in Christ when you heard the word of truth, the gospel of your salvation. Having believed, you were marked in him with a seal, the promised Holy Spirit..."[23]

Of the four necessary elements mentioned by Paul, the evangelist has responsibility only for 'the word of truth'. The calling and mark of the Holy Spirit are God's work, and believing is the responsibility of the one to whom the truth is preached.

Jesus said, "No one can come to me unless the Father who sent me draws him..."[24] So in a very real sense, evangelism is completely dependent on God. Our job is to preach in the hope that those to whom we are preaching are *called* of God.

It must be equally understood that each human being is responsible for his own *reaction* to the gospel, despite the calling of God. Jesus also stated, "For my Father's will is that everyone who looks to the Son and believes in him shall have eternal life..."[25] So despite God's calling and the fact that someone 'looks to the Son', they will not be saved if they do not place faith in Christ. They will remain dead in their sins and

[23] EPHESIANS 1:11-13
[24] JOHN 6:44
[25] JOHN 6:40

condemned at the judgment.

Jesus made these two statements virtually back-to back in John chapter 6, demonstrating that they are not mutually exclusive. God does not make us believe; neither can we believe if God does not prepare our hearts. To be saved, one must be called of the Father *and* believe on the Son.[i]

This being the case, we must make the most of every opportunity we have to allow someone to 'look to the Son'. We need to reveal the complete work of Christ honestly, completely and *scripturally*. Our hearers need to understand the why and how of the gospel so they can make an informed, mature, reasoned decision to place faith in Christ. Otherwise, we may squander an opportunity for them to respond while under God's calling or lead them to respond in a way that does not assure salvation. We are only responsible for what we preach. This makes it of utmost importance that we know what we ought to preach.

Many will walk away from the biblical gospel, even as many walked away from Jesus. Some will walk away because God has not prepared them; some because they estimate the cost of believing is too high. All of this is out of our hands and completely in keeping with what the scripture teaches. We must understand that this is not failure, but the sovereign will of God at work.

When we do not understand this, it is easy for us to begin to push merely for decisions, basing our success on the number of people who respond to our message, when our concern should be to preach resolute truth. A person who is called by God and believes the biblical gospel will have a changed heart at conversion and his life will show it. The person making a 'decision for Christ' by responding with wrong motives to a message of human wisdom will show very little interest in the things of God. The road that modern Christianity travels is littered with people who made 'decisions' for Christ for all the wrong reasons and ended up heart-broken and bitter, "worse off at the end than they were at the beginning"[26]. Out of love for Christ and humanity, we must stop doing this.

The understanding of God's calling has a further effect of strengthening the believer. Consider these words of Paul:

"For those God foreknew he also predestined to be conformed to the likeness of his Son, that he might be the firstborn among many brothers. And those he predestined, he also called; those he called, he also justified; those he justified, he also glorified."[27]

For one reason or another, we have come to think of the idea that God chooses whom He will save as abhorrent. I think that it is because acceptance of the fact that God chooses or elects

[26] 2 PETER 2:20
[27] ROMANS 8:29 & 30

certain individuals for salvation also implies that he sets apart some for wrath. Paul says, "God has mercy on whom he wants to have mercy, and he hardens whom he wants to harden."[28] Hard teaching, I know. But consider what we have given up by refusing this truth.

Think about what it means for God to have foreknown, predestined, called, and justified you. Would there ever be any occasion to doubt your salvation? Could you possibly doubt having known all of this? How many professed believers have fallen away or been consigned to an ineffective life because of doubt? How can we have any confidence in a salvation that depends more on our thoughts and actions than it does God's mercy?

If God does all of this (foreknow, predestine, call, and justify) and we are faithful to preach the truth so that the unsaved fully understand redemption, is God not faithful and powerful enough to complete what He has started? If *He* glorifies those whom He justifies, what more can we do by following them around to see how they are doing? If we need to follow them, or they need to follow us, it should be obvious that they are not following Him. If God has saved them, they are saved. The ones to be concerned about are those who were won by human wisdom and instructed in human regulations, and yet have not truly been justified.

[28] ROMANS 9:18

Paul understood this completely. Whatever we become in Christ, we become because of God's work in our lives. He told the Ephesian church:

> "...we are God's workmanship, created in Christ Jesus to do good works, *which God prepared in advance for us to do.*"[29]

When we come to faith in Christ through the truth of the scriptural gospel, we become God's own workmanship, a new creation in Christ Jesus. He saves us to do good works which are pleasing to Him and bring glory to Him. Scripture says He has actually prepares an individualized follow-up plan for us in advance of our salvation.

Who Will Believe?

While The Bible identifies the atoning sacrifice of Christ as the only way to a relationship with God the Father, we must be careful not to think that it applies to all men at all times. This makes it far too easy to think we are failing when people don't respond to the gospel and to become careless with the message we preach. It seems clear that Paul wanted us to understand that there would be some who would believe and some who wouldn't. In the following verses, he uses belief as the qualifier for salvation. As you read each one, mentally remove the words 'who believe' and see how drastically the meanings are

[29] EPHESIANS 2:10

changed:

> "I am not ashamed of the gospel, because it is the power
> of God for the salvation of everyone *who believes*: first for
> the Jew, then for the Gentile."[30]

> "This righteousness from God comes through faith in
> Jesus Christ to all *who believe*."[31]

> "Christ is the end of the law so that there may be
> righteousness for everyone *who believes*." [32]

> "God was pleased through the foolishness of what was
> preached to save those *who believe*." [33]

Paul goes to great pains to clarify who it is who will be
saved; those *who will believe*. Inversely, there are also those who
will not believe, so the fact that people do not respond to the
message is not an indication of evangelistic failure. Our goal is
not success (which we cannot have without God's sovereign
intervention) so much as it is faithfulness to the message we
have been given.

The belief of which Paul is speaking of is not a conjured up
faith;

> "For it is by grace you have been saved, through faith —
> and this is not from yourselves, it is the gift of God — not

[30] ROMANS 1:16
[31] ROMANS 3:22
[32] ROMANS 10:4
[33] 1 CORINTHIANS 1:21B

by works, so that no one can boast."[34]

Our faith is the gift of God – there is nothing we can do to create it. We cannot push people into it, because it is not of human origin nor is it humanly possible to believe in this way. Anything we have to force on someone is not the faith of which The Bible speaks, and those who are pushed into a decision are very likely to exhibit a tendency toward religion instead of faith, if they do not fall away completely. Biblical belief represents a moment in time in which we finally recognize the wisdom of God as wisdom rather than utter foolishness. As my wife says, it is an 'Aha!' moment. So it is obvious that the evangelist has the sole responsibility of communicating the truth of God with scriptural accuracy so that there may be something substantive of God for the hearer to respond to.

Paul said, "I planted the seed, Apollos watered it, but God made it grow. So neither he who plants nor he who waters is anything, but only God, who makes things grow."[35] We don't know which function we are performing when we preach, but that doesn't matter. When we plant seed, we are faithful. When we water, we are faithful. "The man who plants and the man who waters have one purpose, and each will be rewarded according to his own labor."[36] The fact is that success in evangelism "does not, therefore, depend on man's desire or

[34] EPHESIANS 2:8-9
[35] 1 CORINTHIANS 1:6-7
[36] 1 CORINTHIANS 1:8

effort, but on God's mercy."[37]

Remember the words we long to hear Jesus say on the other side are 'Well done, good and *faithful* servant'[38], not 'good and successful servant'. If we are faithful, God *will* be successful as He pleases, because it is He who calls and He who opens hearts to our preaching, and He who saves.

Just about every effective evangelist in history believed that all of evangelism was God's work; that God is sovereign in evangelism as he is in all else. The Bible teaches that the message is from Him, the messenger is sent by Him; even the Faith by which one believes is from Him. It seems counterintuitive, but knowing that God has placed a calling on some people's lives makes the evangelist more eager to preach. It's just as if the harvest were ripe and all we have to do is go pick the low-hanging fruit.

Yes, No, Maybe

It would seem that there are really only two possible responses to the gospel, 'Yes' or 'No'. But The Bible reveals that there is actually a third kind of response, which we might call 'Maybe'. One of the strongest reasons to preach the scriptural gospel is that the likelihood of creating the 'Maybe' response is greatly reduced. Let's look to the scripture for an explanation of

[37] ROMANS 9:16
[38] MATTHEW 25:21, 25:23

what I mean by 'Maybe'.

In Matthew 22, Jesus relates a parable about a king who prepares a wedding banquet and invites quests to attend. He teaches through this parable several inescapable truths about evangelism.

First, there are many who are invited who will reject the invitation out rightly, as represented by the guests who ignored the invitation and went about other, 'more important' business. It goes without saying that they do so to their own destruction. These are the 'No' camp.

Second, some who are invited will gladly accept the invitation, will prepare themselves for the banquet, and will enter with the blessing of the host. This is the 'Yes' camp.

Finally, there will be those who accept the invitation without counting the cost, as represented by the man who was found without wedding clothes. This 'party crasher', who accepted the invitation gladly but with no intention of changing, is over-represented in our churches today by those who are in the 'Maybe' camp. I place the blame for this on the invitations that we issue.

In the context of the parable, the king has sent his servants out a third time to try and get people to come to the banquet. It's purely conjecture, but I can imagine that the servants are thinking, "At this point I am willing to do whatever I can to get some people into that banquet hall." So rather than issue the invitation as the king had dictated they soften it up. They drop a few of the requirements. They say, "Come to the banquet. Enjoy the food. Enjoy the fellowship. Enjoy the fun." But they fail warn their guests that the host demands that they prepare themselves as appropriate for a wedding banquet. So as this man sits among the other guests enjoying the banquet, the king comes along and sees that he has not prepared himself for the occasion, and orders that he be cast from his presence.[39] So it shall be with the church.

Many of the parables give evidence of the 'Maybe' group. The wheat and the tares, the good fish and the bad fish[40], and the houses on the rock and the sand[41] all speak of these false converts, which live right alongside the true. If you analyze the parables carefully, you will see that Jesus was not contrasting believers with the unbelievers, but true and false converts alongside one another in the church.[ii] He frequently says that they are all 'in the Kingdom' together. The shame is that this 'Maybe' group will not know that they are false believers until it is too late, when "the Son of Man will send out his angels, and they will weed out of his kingdom everything that causes sin and all who do evil."[42] At that point, there will be only sheep

[39] MATTHEW 22:13
[40] SEE MATTHEW 13
[41] SEE MATTHEW 7
[42] MATTHEW 13:41

and goats.[43]

What is even more shameful is that we are the cause of much of it. In our excitement to 'get them into the banquet hall', we will say and do almost anything to entice them. We lower the standard, abandon the righteous requirements of God, and do not warn them to count the cost of discipleship. If we would only issue the invitation as the King has given it, so much of this could be avoided and so many lives spared.

As an example, during a recent revival I attended, a number of people responded to the alter call. The message fell far short of the biblical gospel, and it was the typical 'every head bowed, every eye closed' invitation. I have no way of knowing what actually went on in people's hearts that day, but I would guess that this is perhaps the second or third alter call to which some of them have responded. Some might say that if ten percent of those who responded were actually saved, that is a good thing. In my own opinion, it would be far better to have preached the biblical gospel and have the same ten percent (whom God has called) respond without potentially leading the others into a false religious experience and gospel-hardening them.

Narrow-Minded

Jesus frequently contrasts wide and narrow passages; the

---

[43] SEE MATTHEW 25

wide and narrow gates[44], the narrow road[45], the narrow door[46]. We need to understand that his earthly ministry, his message of the Kingdom, was primarily to the lost sheep of Israel.[47] And that message was a message about true versus false religion, not religion versus irreligion. He spoke to highly religious Jews when he told them to enter by the narrow gate, signifying that those entering the wide gate were not only irreligious 'sinners' but self-righteous religious people as well. The wide road was populated by those who refused to acknowledge God and those who practiced hypocrisy as they twisted His law and burrowed more deeply into their false worship. Though very religious, they would have none of what Jesus offered, which was God's righteousness. They were too full of their own.

Unfortunately, this is still common in our churches today, in large part because the message we preach does not have any provision to break self-righteousness. When we preach a message that brings a sinner to works-righteous religion we move him from the world's superhighway of sin into the wide road, which, though it makes a deceptive promise of heaven, still leads to hell. Once he is on that road it will be substantially harder for him to turn back and find the narrow road.

Paul uses an illustration from Israel's history as a warning

---

[44] MATTHEW 7:13
[45] MATTHEW 7:14
[46] LUKE 13:24
[47] MATTHEW 15:24

that false religion can be hard to detect:

> "For I do not want you to be ignorant of the fact, brothers, that our forefathers were *all* under the cloud and that they *all* passed through the sea. They were *all* baptized into Moses in the cloud and in the sea. They *all* ate the same spiritual food and drank the same spiritual drink; for they drank from the spiritual rock that accompanied them, and that rock was Christ. Nevertheless, God was not pleased with most of them; their bodies were scattered over the desert."[48]

False converts may have experiences similar to true believers. They respond to an invitation, profess faith, are baptized, attend church, give, teach, and do many good things, just as all Israel had shared experiences. But if these things are done from self-righteousness, rather than Christ-righteousness, God is not pleased with them. Not everyone who says to Jesus "Lord, Lord" in the last day will be saved. To the shock of many he will say, "I never knew you. Away from me, you evildoers!"[49]

Jesus completes the parable of the wedding banquet with this sobering statement: "For many are invited, but few are chosen."[50] It is apparent then that we must depend on God for the response to His gospel, because it is He who chooses. We are only responsible to issue the correct invitation. We must tell

[48] 1 CORINTHIANS 10:1-5
[49] MATTHEW 7:21-23
[50] MATTHEW 22:14

them to enter the narrow gate.

Conclusion

There is a very powerful gospel message which God has provided for us to use to His glory. It is a gospel of secret Godly wisdom which transcends the abilities of the one who preaches it and retains its power regardless of the motive of the messenger, and it is demanding enough to turn away those who would be false converts. God is calling people every day to His kingdom, ready to display the power of the Holy Spirit in their lives if they only *hear* and *respond* to His message. So how will they hear?

PREACHING

HOW, THEN, CAN THEY CALL ON THE ONE THEY HAVE NOT BELIEVED IN? AND HOW CAN THEY BELIEVE IN THE ONE OF WHOM THEY HAVE NOT HEARD? AND HOW CAN THEY HEAR WITHOUT SOMEONE PREACHING TO THEM?

ROMANS 10:14

God has ordained one method by which the powerful message he has given His church is to be propagated; preaching.

Strong's Greek dictionary defines the Greek word kērussō, translated in Romans 10:14 (NIV) as preaching, as 'to herald (as a public crier), especially divine truth'. When you preach, you should be publicly declaring God's truth, whether through one-on-one personal evangelism, street preaching, or pulpit preaching. This is God's plan for the advancement His kingdom.

What Preaching is Not

There are other ways of witnessing in addition preaching. Your personal testimony is a witness, your lifestyle is undoubtedly also a witness to the world, and apologetics may be used to bring someone to an intellectual acknowledgment of God. But it must be understood that none of these are the gospel. The gospel is a very specific message which God has provided for the purpose of bringing people to the truth of His kingdom. When we fish for men, these things are merely the bait that encloses the sharp hook of the gospel.

Personal testimony can be a powerful tool in evangelism, but does not take the place of preaching the gospel. In the account of Jesus at Jacob's well in John Chapter 4, Jesus prophetically recounts to a Samaritan woman her adulterous lifestyle. Recognizing that he is a prophet, she returns to her village and proceeds to share testimony of her encounter with Jesus:

> "Then, leaving her water jar, the woman went back to the town and said to the people, 'Come, see a man who told me everything I ever did. Could this be the Messiah?' They came out of the town and made their way toward him."[1]

> "Many of the Samaritans from that town believed in him because of the woman's testimony, 'He told me everything I ever did.' So when the Samaritans came to him, they urged him to stay with them, and he stayed two days. And because of his words many more became be-

[1] JOHN 4:28-30

lievers."[2]

Were the villagers convinced by her testimony, or did the testimony simply lead them to Christ and the gospel? Verse 42 is telling:

> "They said to the woman, 'We no longer believe just because of what you said; now we have heard for ourselves, and we know that this man really is the Savior of the world.'"

Though they believed he was a prophet based on the woman's testimony, the words of Christ led them to know that he was 'the Savior of the World'.

Personal testimony may convince someone of God's power, but "faith comes from hearing the message, and the message is heard through the word of [or 'about'] Christ."[3] I do not want someone to believe on Christ because of what he has done in my life, but because of who he is. I can use my personal testimony to draw them to the gospel, but only through the gospel will they come to fully acknowledge him as savior.

The Chicken or the Egg

What we currently call 'lifestyle evangelism' should not be thought of as evangelism at all, but as living out the call of the gospel. There is no doubt that we must lead a life that pleases

2 JOHN 4:39-41
3 ROMANS 10:17

God before outsiders, however we shouldn't do it primarily for the sake of outsiders but for the sake of God. If we live in a way that pleases God, we will naturally be very different from those in the world. Jesus said, "Let *your* light shine before others, that they may see your good deeds and glorify your Father in heaven."[4] The light should be something which we already possess and a natural, continuous expression of our love for God, not something we put on as a show for outsiders. We are called to *be* a peculiar people, not *act like* a peculiar people.[5]

The true gospel readily acknowledges that we are all sinners whether we are believers or unbelievers. Lifestyle evangelism puts the cart before the horse by expecting us to put on righteousness for the world to see that will lead them to seek what we have. It is dangerous in that it can cause us to conform to an outward righteousness without changing our hearts, which is the very thing that the unbelieving around us suspect and abhor.

Is it possible that gospel preaching leads to gospel living and not vice-versa? Looking back to the first chapter, we will remember that Paul began to preach immediately after his conversion in Damascus. He was preaching in the synagogues of the city to people who knew his reputation as a man who arrested believers so that they might be imprisoned or put to

---

[4] MATTHEW 5:16
[5] 1 PETER 2:9 (KJV)

death. "All those who heard him were astonished and asked, 'Isn't he the man who raised havoc in Jerusalem among those who call on this name?'"[6]

In the modern church, we often give young believers the impression that they need to clean up their act before they begin preaching. We wouldn't dream of sending a new convert out to preach the gospel if his reputation were as bad as Paul's. We would demand some time for 'maturing' first, so he didn't frighten away all the potential converts. We are very fortunate that Paul never gave anyone the chance to persuade him to 'mature' before he began his preaching ministry.

It seems to me that if we teach young Christians how to get out and share their faith, to go among those whom they know need the Lord and preach His powerful message, their lives will be far more dynamic. Preaching gives you something to live up to. If you are publically declaring the gospel, your community becomes your accountability partner.

Paul sums this idea up rather succinctly in his first letter to the Corinthians. "I beat my body and make it my slave so that after I have preached to others, I myself will not be disqualified for the prize."[7] In other words, he is not going to live his life in a manner that will compromise his witness or endanger his standing with God, because to do so will affect (potentially de-

[6] ACTS 9:21
[7] I CORINTHIANS 9:27

stroy) many, many lives. Notice the order in which he presents his thoughts; he disciplines his body because he *has* preached the gospel, not so that he can preach the gospel. The old adage 'practice what you preach' is often used to scold hypocrites. But in truth, preaching the gospel will bring the knowledge and desire to practice gospel living.

As C.H. Spurgeon once said, "If you are saved yourself, the work is but half done until you are employed to bring others to Christ." I am convinced that this is the very reason that I remained an infant Christian for twenty-plus years. I *never* shared my faith because I did not understand the gospel, though I professed to be a Christian. I was also afraid that my lifestyle witness was not strong enough to allow me to do so. When I began to preach it changed me deeply. I found that I was always searching for ideas that I could use to clearly express the grace of God to others, and those thoughts began to profoundly renew my own mind and open the scriptures to me in ways I had never imagined. But this only started once I quit *trying* to clean up my act and just surrendered to preaching. I think it is a sad thing when people say that they could never preach to anyone because they do not consider themselves to be good enough to speak into other's lives. This demonstrates a limited understanding of the power of the gospel. It is God, not ourselves, that makes us competent as ministers of the new covenant. The only difference between believers and unbelievers is grace, which is the only thing we have that is worth sharing.

Poor in Spirit

There is a movement beginning in the church today that is seeking to draw Christians back to a simpler lifestyle. It emphasizes the joy of helping others over self-satisfaction. Many are downsizing their lives, abandoning the American dream to give their time, energy and money for the Kingdom of God. These are excellent works, but we must never start to think that preaching is unnecessary because we are showing the love of the Lord by our works.

The unsaved cannot 'catch' salvation from exposure to Christians. Stop for a minute and think about how you were saved. Did you say to yourself, "Joe Christian over there is sure a nice guy, I want to be just like him", or was Joe Christian bold enough to tell you about what Christ had done for you, so you could understand it and put your faith in Him? No matter how pleasant and helpful and compassionate you are, unless you preach the gospel, no one will be truly saved. Your lifestyle is a witness; it is not the gospel. The gospel is what people must *hear*, *understand* and *believe* to be saved, so while we may do all of these things out of love for God and others, we still must preach.

The danger in this type of teaching is that it can cause us to focus our attention exclusively on those in society whom we deem 'misfortunate'. We can mistakenly begin to think that the gospel appeals only to those who have been reduced to desperation by worldly circumstances, when in reality it is meant to appeal to those who recognize their spiritual poverty. While the poor and downtrodden definitely have need of the gospel, so do the wealthy and the intellectually elite. Since the gospel deals specifically with righteousness and not necessarily wealth, happiness or success in this life, no one is immune from the need for it. There is no one righteous, not even one.[8] Whether rich or poor, happy or broken, we are all Adam's descendants, and all need the savior.

Some will say, "Didn't Jesus spend his time among the poor and unfortunate?" Yes. But he also spent time with Nicodemas, the Roman Centurion and Zacchaeus, men of means and influence. He was an equal opportunity savior, and no respecter of persons. Jesus spent time with those who had *humble* hearts. Fortunately for us, God has given us provision in the gospel to bring humility to the sinner as we shall learn later.

Jesus spent time with those who were humble enough to realize they needed him; they often happened to be the misfortunate. And he didn't do it to give them a helping hand or to impress them with his kindness. He did it so that he might have the opportunity to *preach* the truths of the kingdom to

8 ROMANS 3:10

them. His ministry of healing was not just for the sake of healing, but so that the message of the Kingdom could be furthered. Look at the 'beatitudes' in chapter 5 of Matthew's gospel:

Blessed are the poor in spirit

Blessed are those who mourn

Blessed are the meek

Blessed are those who hunger and thirst for righteousness

Blessed are the merciful

Blessed are the pure in heart

Blessed are the peacemakers

Blessed are those who are persecuted because of righteousness

It seems that Jesus spent his time among the blessed ones, regardless of their place in the world. That they were prostitutes and sinners made no difference so long as they hungered and thirsted for righteousness. That they were of the hated Roman army was of little consequence if they were meek. They were all accepted by Jesus because they were all *humble* enough to accept him and his words.

Simplifying our lives and downsizing our possessions is an excellent idea. Spending more time concentrating on what God wants from us and less time worrying about what we want for ourselves is completely scriptural. Loving those around us is exactly what Jesus did and taught. But what God wants most from us and the most loving thing we can do for those around us (in fact the very thing that Jesus did) is to share the truth of the gospel with them.

Meaningful Relationships

This leads into the concept of 'relationship evangelism'. We have been taught in recent years that we must establish a relationship with someone, befriend them and gain their trust before we can share the gospel with them. So popular is this idea that many people now speak as if this is the only way that we can properly evangelize.

But there are several serious flaws inherent in relational evangelism. First and foremost, what if the person dies in their sin before we ever get to tell them about Christ? If it takes a year, two years or more for us to feel like we have earned the right to speak into their lives, they may no longer be around to hear us.

Second, by the time we've invested in a friendship, we may be afraid to share our faith because it will jeopardize a relationship that took so long to build.

Finally, and most importantly, it is just not biblical. Jesus himself gave specific instructions to his disciples about preaching the gospel. He told them, "If anyone will not welcome you or listen to your words, leave that home or town and shake the dust off your feet"[9], implying that they should first preach and then look for a reaction, the inverse of relationship evangelism. Time will not change an unbeliever's innate disdain for God's righteousness, but it is an enemy to the unrepentant who have a rather short lifetime in which to decide to obey the gospel or face God's wrath. The very fact that those around us will face wrath, if we believe it, should create a sense of urgency that excludes lifestyle and relational evangelism.

We have become convinced that sharing the gospel is a slow, gradual process. In scripture, the gospel is never open-ended. You may not be able to identify consciously when it came to you, but it is a definite event, not a process. Biblically, it asks a direct, pointed question. The gospel says, "Here are the facts, will you believe or not? Here are the wide and narrow gates. Enter the narrow gate." This is how Jesus preached. He didn't walk up to his disciples thinking, "I will be friends with these guys so when they get to the point that they trust me I can share the secrets of the Kingdom with them." No. He said, in effect, "Leave all you have and come follow me..." making his intentions clear at the beginning of the relationship. Some followed and some didn't, but they all knew where they stood.

In Mark chapter 10, we find the story of the rich young man

9 MATTHEW 10:14

who approached Jesus seeking how he might inherit eternal life. This is an evangelist's dream, having someone approach you and ask you how they might be saved. Jesus asks the young man if he has kept the commandments, and the response is "Teacher, all these I have kept from my youth."[10] Scripture then tells us that 'Jesus, looking at him, loved him'.[11] Out of love for the man, Jesus did not simply invite him to come along and imitate his grace. He asked him to first give up the very thing that was most precious to him; his riches. There is no indication that Jesus tried to ease him into the Kingdom hoping that he would become a follower; he frequently imposed difficult demands on those who would follow him. This young man went away sorrowful because he loved his riches more than he did eternal life. Jesus made immediately clear what the gospel demanded as a prerequisite to a relationship with him, despite his love for the man and the sincerity of the man's question.

Gospel?

In the preceding pages, I described just about every kind of "evangelism" that is popular today. The prevalent attitude of the church is that we are to love sinners into a relationship with Christ, and in the following chapters we will look at scriptural truth that explains why none of this *really* works.

It is probably not fair to say that we have lost confidence in

[10] MARK 10:20 (ESV)
[11] MARK 10:21 (ESV)

the gospel, because I don't think most of us know what the gospel actually is. If we could understand the depth of the freedom that we have in Christ through the grace of God expressed in the good news of the gospel, we could express that to one another and to those outside the church in the way that Paul did, without shame, without trickery, without spending thousands of hours involved in things that never amount to very much. As you grasp the tone of Paul's writing, you realize that the gospel was not a touchy-feely thing with Paul. It was a firmly established fact – one which he was obligated to preach.

Much Obliged

Over the last 100 years the church has tried anything and everything to get out of having to preach the gospel truth. Completely neglecting the direct command of Jesus, we have hidden behind politics, bumper stickers, t-shirts, slogans, boycotts and anything else that would allow us a convenient excuse not to preach. We have done a careful job of searching the scripture for any nuance that might release us from our obligation to preach, while completely ignoring the literal injunction of God to do so.

Jesus told his disciples to "Go into all the world and preach the good news to all creation."[12] That was their calling and ours; the reason we are left here. Yet it seems that we are interested in

[12] MARK 16:15

everything but that calling. Go into your local Christian bookstore and ask to see the evangelism section. If they have one, it is probably comprised of six titles. Now compare that to the Christian romance novel section. That says a lot about the modern church.

It seems odd to me in light of the Great Commission that we tend to hold those who are actively involved in evangelism in high esteem, as if they are the 'hyperspiritual'. Many say, "I could never just walk up to a stranger and start preaching." Why not? We are all commanded to preach by the Lord and we all have the same resources available with which to carry out his commandment. The lack of self-confidence is a good thing because preaching is all about confidence in the power of God. Without question, we are all obligated to preach. So why don't we?

Paul preached out of a deep sense of obligation. He was obliged to preach to all he came in contact with.[13] He made it his life's work, but did not consider himself special because of it:

"Yet when I preach the gospel, I cannot boast, for I am compelled to preach. Woe to me if I do not preach the gospel! If I preach voluntarily, I have a reward; if not voluntarily, I am simply discharging the trust committed

---

[13] SEE ROMANS 1:14

to me."[14]

Simply discharging a trust? No Holy Ghost goose bumps? Woe to me if I do not preach? That sounds almost like legalism. He plainly understood that he was here for a reason, and that in fulfilling his calling he was doing nothing extraordinary. Having done everything he was told to do, he had only done his duty as an unworthy servant.[15]

Although evangelism is the exception in the church today, by all rights it should be the rule. Paul wrote to Timothy, at Ephesus in a pastoral role, "But you, keep your head in all situations, endure hardship, do the work of an evangelist, discharge all the duties of your ministry."[16] Surely Timothy's duties were as staggering as those of any modern pastor; teacher, overseer, marrying, burying and counseling among hundreds of others. Paul doesn't list any of these; he simply admonishes Timothy to 'discharge the duties of his ministry'. But he specifically tells him to 'do the work of an evangelist'.

We have become so busy in church activity, so focused on our own little area of specialized ministry, that we no longer consider it our duty to do the work of an evangelist. We think that evangelism is a special calling that requires a unique gifting from God. It has become easy for us to use the business of our ministry as an excuse *not* to do evangelistic work. But truth be

[14] 1 CORINTHIANS 9:16-17
[15] LUKE 17:7-10
[16] 2 TIMOTHY 4:5

told, if any ministry in the church does not have as its primary focus the winning of souls, it is not a ministry. You might call it a work or a hobby, but it is not a ministry. We are all called to the work of the evangelist, whether we realize it and accept it or not. Every ministry of the church ought always to have an eye toward the cross, not haphazardly hoping for an opportunity to share the gospel, but designed and executed to make as many opportunities as possible to do so. Then we have to *seize* those opportunities.

The next time you are tempted to think that your ministry keeps you too busy to allow time for evangelism, picture Paul dictating a letter to a companion in near darkness. He has a little apostolic ministry to deal with, you know. No big deal, he just oversees most of the churches in the known world by way of messengers because he is imprisoned in a Roman dungeon. He is preparing a letter to the church at Ephesus. You or I might have begged them to pray for our release from prison, for better food, better air, or clean water. He had one prayer request for himself; "Pray also for me, that whenever I open my mouth, words may be given me so that I will fearlessly make known the mystery of the gospel, for which I am an ambassador in chains. Pray that I may declare it fearlessly, as I should."[17] The man clearly had his ministry priorities straight.

If we are unworthy servants for having done all that we were

[17] EPHESIANS 6:19-20

told to do, what are we if we don't do even that much? We need to stop using excuses and trying to take shortcuts and start *preaching*. I know the term preaching has a negative connotation these days, but The Bible certainly does not teach that. It teaches that preaching is the lifeblood of the faith.

The Foolishness of Preaching

If you think that preaching is foolishness, you are in good company. Paul stated:

"For since in the wisdom of God the world through its wisdom did not know him, God was pleased through the foolishness of what was preached to save those who believe."[18]

Did you hear that? How does God save those who believe? Through the foolishness of what is preached. There is no getting around it – God has established a Kingdom that is expanded *only* by the foolishness of preaching. So why do we spend so much time praying for revival and kingdom growth, and so little time preaching?

It is widely accepted that only about 2% of evangelical church members in America share their faith regularly and actively. Breaking it down even further, some unknown portion of those are actually involved in 'the preaching of foolishness'

---

[18] 1 CORINTHIANS 1:21

(the wisdom of the world) rather than 'the foolishness of preaching' (the wisdom of God). I am afraid that they are winning. If the gospel is God's power to save and keep those who hear and believe it (as scripture claims) is it any wonder that those who hear and believe something that sounds like the gospel and yet is not live powerless, ineffective lives?

If Spurgeon was correct when he said "Have you no wish for others to be saved? Then you are not saved yourself" and it is true that only 2% *actively* share their faith, then why are the other 98% even attending church? This is food for thought.

The American Dream

American Christianity is an interesting mix. The church I attend is pretty heavily involved in overseas mission work. One of the greatest fears of those who are invested in such work is that Christ will become to the targeted peoples just 'another god', lumped on top of animistic beliefs and ideologies from other world religions.

A while back God convicted me of the fact that we never really worry about this when we speak with those of our own nation. We often times preach a gospel in which we take Christ and tack him onto the 'American dream'; our political, moral, financial and cultural beliefs. Our gospel is as American as apple pie; it packs all the spiritual punch of a Norman Rockwell cover illustration.

We make a habit of trying to twist scripture to impose our American values on it. We will condemn with worldly authority such things as homosexuality, abortion, taxes and the school system, yet shy away from preaching the hard truth of the biblical gospel. Rather than preaching the gospel of Jesus Christ, our American brand of Christianity has us sitting around browbeating people about perceived injustice and true moral decay as our neighbors slip quietly into hell.

The truly amazing thing about this is we are the only ones who don't recognize it. We have long been branded the 'religious right' and seem to be okay with it. It is as if we don't realize that this is how our neighbors perceive us – not as agents of truth in a lost world, but as a fanatical political faction motivated by religion. Incredibly, we can be very bold and vocal (even obnoxious) about our moral opinions, yet remain completely moot on the gospel.

I am sure that this is in part due to our relativistic 'Americanized' gospel; the message to which we respond tends to shape our concept of what it means to be a Christian. We are the Currier and Ives of Christendom; all warm and homey and sentimental without an ounce of power. That is also the message we preach. To me it is clear that we cannot continue to behave this way and expect to make any significant impact for Christ in this nation.

Conclusion

We need to start preaching and living the gospel truth found in the scriptures, and to do that we must know what that truth is.

The opening scripture in the introduction to this book is 2 Corinthians 10:5. It admonishes us to take every thought captive to make it obedient to Christ; to demolish every argument and pretense that sets itself up against the knowledge of God. Be ready to do that, because in the next chapter I intend to start introducing you to a gospel you may never have heard before.

SEND THE LIGHT!

Paul then stood up in the meeting of the Areopagus and said: "Men of Athens! I see that in every way you are very religious. For as I walked around and looked carefully at your objects of worship, I even found an altar with this inscription: TO AN UNKNOWN GOD. Now what you worship as something unknown I am going to proclaim to you."

ACTS 17:22-23

Most of us look to the third chapter of the Gospel of John to find what is widely considered the most concise biblical definition of the gospel. Specifically verse 16, in which Jesus states "For God so loved the world that he gave his one and only Son, that whoever believes in him shall not perish but have eternal life."

I believe that the fullness of the gospel actually resides in verses 16-21. These verses are all linked together as a single idea that Jesus conveyed, and to look solely at verse 16 can give us a skewed view of what the biblical gospel message actually is. Let's look at these verses:

[16]"For God so loved the world that he gave his one and only Son, that whoever believes in him shall not perish but have eternal life. [17]For God did not send his Son into the world to condemn the world, but to save the world through him. [18]Whoever believes in him is not condemned, but whoever does not believe stands condemned already because he has not believed in the name of God's one and only Son. [19]This is the verdict: Light has come into the world, but men loved darkness instead of light because their deeds were evil. [20]Everyone who does evil hates the light, and will not come into the light for fear that his deeds will be exposed. [21]But whoever lives by the truth comes into the light, so that it may be seen plainly that what he has done has been done through God."

I see in this passage three separate ideas, or steps, which men must follow to come to grace. They are, in reverse order;

1. They must come into the light (verses 19-21)

2. They must recognize their condemnation before God (verses 17-18)

3. They must understand the grace of God (verse 16)

In this chapter we will look, with the help of Paul, at why Jesus said that men must "come into the light"; to move from the realm of natural thought to the realm of spiritual thought, or from lies to truth. In order to understand why this step to grace is necessary, we need to understand something very important about the gospel; it is not and never was intended to be attractive to the prideful, carnal mind.

Hate, Ignorance and Blindness

Look again at verse 20. "Everyone who does evil *hates the light*, and will not come into the light for fear that his deeds will be exposed." God is completely intolerant of sin, and because the biblical gospel was given by God, it also carries a message of intolerance for sin. Jesus here teaches that the light (or the truth, if you will) exposes sin, and because the sinner fears having his deeds exposed, he will not come into the light. In fact, he *hates* the light.

To many of us who have been Christians for many years this idea sounds somewhat foreign. It may even make us a little uncomfortable to think of the gospel in this way. To us the message is glorious. We can all say 'but for the grace of God, there go I'. But scripture takes great pains to remind us that this is not so for those in the darkness.

Jesus uses very strong words here in expressing the attitude of unbelievers toward the gospel. He says that they 'hate the light'. Similarly, in Romans 8:7, Paul tells us that "The sinful mind is hostile to God. It does not submit to God's law, nor can it do so." This is not just ambivalence toward God; this is absolute hatred and outright hostility toward God and his righteous requirements. We often see this acted out in deliberate ways elsewhere in the world; over 170,000 Christians are martyred worldwide each year.[iii] Even in our own nation we recognize that tolerance is extended to virtually every segment of society accept evangelical Christians, almost unconsciously.

In addition to this hatred, the mind of the unbeliever is unable to understand the things of God.

"The man without the Spirit does not accept the things that come from the Spirit of God, for they are foolishness to him, and he cannot understand them, because they are spiritually discerned."[1]

When we walk up to an unbeliever and share John 3:16 with them, nine out of ten times it is utter foolishness to them. The fact that God's son died so that they might be saved has no real bearing on them because they don't have a clue that they need to be saved, let alone from what they need to be saved. From their unspiritual frame of reference, it makes no sense.

In addition to hatred and a lack of understanding, those in the world are spiritually blind. Paul tells us:

---

[1] 1 CORINTHIANS 2:14

"The god of this age has blinded the minds of unbelievers, so that they cannot see the light of the gospel of the glory of Christ, who is the image of God."[2]

They cannot even see the light, so closed are their minds toward God and the truth.

In recent years we have taught and accepted the idea that unbelievers will respond to a message of God's love. As believers and people who know and appreciate the overwhelming love of God, we can have a hard time understanding why it is not an appealing message to the world. But if we accept the biblical reality that people avoid (and even hate) God because they instinctively know that He demands righteousness, that they cannot comprehend spiritual truth, and that their minds are blinded to that truth, we will have to concede that there is no way for them to relate to God's love unless these barriers are removed.

This leaves us two options: we can remove the requirement of righteousness and the deeper spiritual truths from our message in the hope that we can appeal to human understanding (i.e. the modern gospel message) or preach a biblical gospel as Paul did and trust in the message and the Holy Spirit.

[2] 2 CORINTHIANS 4:4

Into the Light

If we are to obey the commandment of Jesus to preach the gospel, we must learn how we are to do it. As we have seen in the preceding pages, the would-be evangelist has an uphill battle in overcoming hatred, ignorance and spiritual blindness before he can even get people to see the need for the savior, let alone place faith in him.

Preaching is supernatural warfare:

"For our struggle is not against flesh and blood, but against the rulers, against the authorities, against the powers of this dark world and against the spiritual forces of evil in the heavenly realms."[3]

The gospel, being a spiritual message, needs to be presented to someone in a spiritual mindset. Rather than trying to bait them to the gospel using temporal or human arguments, we need to create a spiritual ambush of sorts. Because this battle will never be won on Satan's turf, where people are completely deceived, those who are being used by the enemy must be drawn onto God's turf, which is truth. This is the first step to grace.

If unbelievers are to be brought into the light, the church must first bring the light out to them. Considering what The Bible has to say about the spiritual state of the unbeliever, it

[3] EPHESIANS 6:12

seems unlikely that he will ever darken the doorway of a church that preaches a scriptural message. So in order to reach lost people, we need to get out-of-doors and bring the scripture to them. We must go where they are. We needn't go find those who are in worldly need, be it financial, emotional or whatever. All unbelievers are suffering from spiritual poverty, so we need not wait for a tragedy as an excuse to go – the fact that 150,000 people die every day, most of them without knowing Christ, is tragedy enough.

Bringing the light outside of our churches is not enough; we will have to find ways to literally drag people into that light by involving them in conversations about spiritual things. Take the example of Paul on Mars Hill in Athens (see the opening scripture for this chapter). He begins by speaking about the natural things around him and then intentionally pushes the conversation to the spiritual realm. In effect he says, "Folks, I can see that you are religious people because you have built monuments to many gods. I even found one dedicated to an 'unknown god'. Let me tell you about that unknown God!"

Jesus himself uses this technique in John chapter four while speaking with the woman at the well. He starts the conversation by asking her to draw water for him and then turns the conversation to the spiritual idea of living water. He transitions from the realm of natural thought to the realm of spiritual thought. He is turning her thoughts toward heavenly things.

Knock, Knock

Where we have been trained in recent years to wait for opportunities to present the gospel, we can and must learn how to *make* opportunities. We must take the initiative of intentionally going into our communities to preach the gospel, as the early church did. Presenting a good, interesting gospel tract or being ready to ask a penetrating question at an opportune point in a conversation are two ways of turning a conversation to the spiritual.

Tracts are an effective way of sharing the gospel, if they are good quality tracts with a biblical gospel message. I know that many in today's society, even within the church, think that a person standing on the street corner handing out tracts is an oddity, but many have been saved after being handed a tract. Hudson Taylor was a missionary credited with bringing over 18,000 Chinese nationals to the Lord in the 19th century. He was saved while reading a tract he had inadvertently picked up from his father's desk one day while looking for something to occupy his time.

As we engage people in conversations that lead to an opportunity to share the gospel, we need to be aware of how we are being received. A person's manner and body language will indicate if they are comfortable with our presence. Are they interested in the conversation or is it obvious that we are annoying them? We need to know that they are willing to converse with us before we begin a discussion of spiritual things. Jesus said to Nicodemas, "I have spoken to you of earthly things and you do not believe; how then will you believe if I speak of heavenly things?"[4] If the person to whom we are speaking about natural things shows little interest in the conversation, does it make any sense to share eternal truths with them? We want to make sure we have someone's undivided attention before we begin to pry open the door and let in the light.

Unbelievers spend their whole lives trying not to think about death. Death is depressing to them for two reasons; it seems very finite and it forces them to think about what lies beyond. Interestingly, you will find that as a subject of conversation, they are fascinated by it. This is to our advantage.

One of the best ways to force someone to confront spiritual truth without being offensive is to ask a simple question, something like: "Will you go to heaven when you die?" or "What do you think happens to someone after they die?" Either of these questions will confront them with the fact that they will die and the fact that there is something after death. Most

[4] JOHN 3:12

everyone will answer these questions because they all have an opinion. If we listen carefully to the answers they give it can reveal a lot about where they are spiritually.

Keep in mind that just because someone says they are a Christian, it does not mean that they have heard the biblical gospel. There are many who have heard a message and made a 'decision' without ever perceiving the wisdom of God that scripture reveals. When someone tells us that they are a Christian, we can challenge them gently. If they really understand grace, they will appreciate the opportunity to defend and share their faith. We should live our lives "always being prepared to make a defense to anyone who asks you for a reason for the hope that is in you"[5], so we may legitimately suspect that those who cannot give a reason may not have that hope. In a case like this, we can continue to present the gospel to them by 'teaching' them how they can share their faith. Often times, those who claim to be Christian will be the ones most astounded by the scriptural gospel when they finally hear it.

Conclusion

Engaging people in spiritual conversations is not an easy thing to do, but the fact is that it must be done in order to have the opportunity to lead them to the scriptural gospel. This is

[5] 1 PETER 3:15 (ESV)

actually how Jesus most often approached preaching, turning casual conversations to the spiritual and sharing parables to reveal deep truths in simple terms. He then took time with those who showed curiosity to explain the meanings behind the parables in plain terms. In the same way, we must learn to engage people in conversation which may lead to an opportunity to share the gospel truth.

THROWING THE BOOK

THEREFORE NO ONE WILL BE DECLARED RIGHTEOUS IN HIS SIGHT BY OBSERVING THE LAW; RATHER, THROUGH THE LAW WE BECOME CONSCIOUS OF SIN.

ROMANS 3:20

In the last chapter we looked at John 3:19-21, explaining that the first step to grace was for a person to come into the light. Step two is for them to become convinced of their condemnation, based on John 3:18; "Whoever believes in him is not condemned, but whoever does not believe stands condemned already because he has not believed in the name of God's one and only Son." In this chapter we are going to look at evidence that Paul's gospel used the law of God to convince his hearers of their condemnation, and why.

The Law

In various places throughout the New Testament, Paul refers to the law. What law? The Old Testament law which God gave

Israel through Moses, commonly called the Mosaic Law. His generic reference to law refers to both the ceremonial and moral aspects of that law. The moral portion is what we call the Ten Commandments. In Romans 7, Paul says "Indeed I would not have known what sin was except through the law. For I would not have known what coveting really was if the law had not said, 'Do not covet.'"[1] We recognize the phrase 'Do not covet' as the tenth commandment, indicating that when Paul references the law in this part of Romans, he is speaking of the Commandments.

In this same verse (Romans 7:7) Paul makes clear to us what the use of the Old Testament law is; to make us aware of what sin really is - lawlessness.

Back in the chapter on preaching, I discussed moral relativism. This ideology, which is commonplace in the west today, states that what may be wrong for one person may not be wrong for another. This stands in direct contradiction to the law of God, which states that there are things which are always wrong, period. Fortunately God foresaw the problem with moral relevance (or more likely it always existed) and provided us with a means of measuring right and wrong that is external to our own thoughts and beliefs. That standard is the Ten Commandments.

[1] ROMANS 7:7B

On the face of it, pleasing God would appear to be a matter of keeping His standard. It would seem that keeping the Ten Commandments would make you righteous:

1. You shall have no other gods before me

2. You shall not make for yourself an idol

3. You shall not misuse the name of the LORD your God

4. Remember the Sabbath day by keeping it holy

5. Honor your father and your mother

6. You shall not murder

7. You shall not commit adultery

8. You shall not steal

9. You shall not lie

10. You shall not covet

It becomes obvious that this is not so simple when you realize that if you have told one lie (Commandment 9) you have broken the law. If you have broken one part of the law, you have broken the whole, according to scripture.[2]

Jesus magnified the law further, proclaiming that the intent of a person's heart meant more than his outward actions. For

[2] JAMES 2:10

example, the seventh Commandment says 'You shall not commit adultery', but Jesus said "I tell you that anyone who looks at a woman lustfully has already committed adultery with her in his heart."[3] In the New Testament, murder is not defined solely as the outward act of killing, but as John says "Anyone who hates his brother is a murderer..."[4]

The ultimate standard that Jesus gave us is clearly impossible to attain by human effort; "Be perfect, therefore, as your heavenly Father is perfect."[5] To please God, we must be perfect, even as He is perfect.

Beyond all doubt we are destined to fail if we try to keep the letter of the law, let alone the intent. It is impossible to do so, and that is the point. The law was never meant to justify us before God, but to paint us into a corner so we have no place to turn but to God's mercy.

This is the specific job of the law, as stated by Paul in Galatians 3:24; "So the law was put in charge to lead us to Christ that we might be justified by faith." Meditate on that verse for a moment and consider these questions in light of what it says:

1. Is it the love of God that draws us to Christ?

2. Is it the promise of a better life here on earth that

[3] MATTHEW 5:28
[4] 1 JOHN 3:15
[5] MATTHEW 5:48

draws us to Christ?

3. Is it the promise of eternal life that draws us to Christ?

4. Is it sickness, poverty, heartache or addiction that drives us to Christ?

5. Is it the fear of hell that drives us to Christ?

According to Paul, it is the law of God that *leads* us to Christ. This is possibly the most neglected point in modern evangelism, so think it through. To preach a biblical gospel, we must preach the law as well as grace. If we do not preach the law, our hearers cannot know in a biblical sense what sin is, and without knowing that sin is transgression of God's law[6], which justly deserves to be punished, they cannot appreciate the need for a savior. Without the bad news, the good news is absurd. Our job is to introduce them to the law so that *it* can lead them to Christ.

The Proper Use of the Law

Jesus acknowledged that an understanding of the law was critical to one's understanding of the gospel. In Luke chapter 16 we find the parable of Lazarus and the rich man. Lazarus, a beggar, lay at the rich man's gate and begged for scraps during his lifetime. When they both had died, the rich man found

[6] 1JOHN 3:4

himself in Hades seeing Lazarus at Abraham's side in Heaven.

After recognizing his own condemnation, the rich man said to Abraham,

> "I beg you, father, send Lazarus to my family, for I have five brothers. Let him warn them, so that they will not also come to this place of torment."

> "Abraham replied, 'They have Moses and the Prophets; let them listen to them.'"

> "'No, father Abraham,' he said, 'but if someone from the dead goes to them, they will repent.'"

> "He [Abraham] said to him, 'If they do not listen to Moses and the Prophets, they will not be convinced even if someone rises from the dead.'"

If the law, which appeals to the conscience, and fulfilled prophecy, which appeals to the intellect, cannot lead a person to repentance, neither will the resurrection of the dead. In telling this parable, Jesus was not discounting what he was to do on the cross, but pointing out that no miracle alone will convince a person of his sin. That is the job of Moses and the Prophets.

The vast majority of people believe that they are 'good' enough to earn a place in heaven. This can mean one of two things; either they are ignorant of God's law and don't know what sin really is, or they believe they have kept His law. Most in our society are ignorant of the law, but what about someone who claims to have kept the law? Can he be justified by his works?

Paul tells us over and over again in his writings that justification is not a lawful use of the law. The law has no power to justify. Consider these verses:

"We know that the law is good if one uses it properly. We also know that law is made not for the righteous but for lawbreakers…"[7]

"Therefore no one will be declared righteous in his sight by observing the law; rather, through the law we become conscious of sin."[8]

"So we, too, have put our faith in Christ Jesus that we may be justified by faith in Christ and not by observing the law, because by observing the law no one will be justified."[9]

"I do not set aside the grace of God, for if righteousness could be gained through the law, Christ died for nothing!"[10]

"For if a law had been given that could impart life, then

[7] 1 TIMOTHY 1:8 & 9
[8] ROMANS 3: 20
[9] GALATIANS 2:16
[10] GALATIANS 2:21

righteousness would certainly have come by the law."[11]

He also makes it clear that righteousness comes from God, by grace, and not through the law:

"But now a righteousness from God, apart from law, has been made known, to which the Law and the Prophets testify. This righteousness from God comes through faith in Jesus Christ to all who believe. There is no difference, for all have sinned and fall short of the glory of God, and are justified freely by his grace through the redemption that came by Christ Jesus."[12]

None of us can be justified by the law because all have sinned and fall short of the standard. It makes no difference whether we are ignorant of the law or trying to keep the law – all have sinned and need the grace of God. If we say we haven't sinned, we make God out to be a liar.[13]

Even if it were possible for us to keep the whole of the law, that would merely be self-righteousness. The Bible makes it clear that our own righteousness is less than worthless in God's sight. To Him, "all our righteous acts are like filthy rags"[14]. We must be saved by His grace, through faith. So tainted by sin are we that Paul tells us even our faith is "not from yourselves, it is

[11] GALATIANS 3:21
[12] ROMANS 3:21-24
[13] 1 JOHN 1:10
[14] ISAIAH 64:6

the gift of God — not by works, so that no one can boast."[15] We are so full of self-righteousness that we can't even produce faith that pleases God. Remember John 3:18; "whoever does not believe stands condemned already because he has not believed in the name of God's one and only Son." In reality, it is not even lawlessness that condemns the unrepentant sinner, but his refusal of the Son of God. If it were possible for us by force of will to keep the law perfectly, we would still be condemned because our works would come from our sinful nature. As Paul said, "Those controlled by the sinful nature cannot please God."[16] The the writer of Hebrews adds, "…without faith it is impossible to please God…"[17]

The proper use of the law is to help mankind realize how we measure up to God's standard – to make us conscious of our sin. Our nature is to want to compare ourselves with others, but the biblical gospel - through the use of the law - forces us to compare ourselves with the unchanging standard by which God judges sin.

As My Gospel Declares

Now that we have an understanding of the proper use of the law, we may wonder what evidence there is that Paul used it in

[15] EPHESIANS 2:8 & 9
[16] ROMANS 8:8
[17] HEBREWS 11:6

presenting his gospel. Since we have little of Paul's gospel preaching recorded, how do we know he used the law in declaring the gospel?

First, he asserts himself that had it not been for the law, he would not have known what sin was (Romans 7:7). He surely would have wanted his hearers to have a clear understanding of sin. That in addition to the other writings we have looked at juxtaposing the law with grace would seem to indicate that this was an important part of Paul's gospel. He stated that it is the law that leads a sinner to Christ, which is the main purpose of evangelism. So we might safely assume that Paul preached law.

As we learned in the first chapter of the book, Paul was "entrusted with the gospel to the uncircumcised, just as Peter had been entrusted with the gospel to the circumcised…"[18] Why would there be a separate gospel for each group? The obvious difference would be a familiarity with the law of God, which the Jews possessed and the Gentiles did not. Again, it stands to reason that Paul's message must introduce his Gentile hearers to the law before he can lead them to an understanding of grace.

In Romans chapter two, Paul gives us a very important but easily missed clue as to his use of the law in evangelism. Let's look at verses 12-16:

[18] GALATIANS 2:7(ESV)

[12]All who sin apart from the law will also perish apart from the law, and all who sin under the law will be judged by the law. [13]For it is not those who hear the law who are righteous in God's sight, but it is those who obey the law who will be declared righteous. [14](Indeed, when Gentiles, who do not have the law, do by nature things required by the law, they are a law for themselves, even though they do not have the law, [15]since they show that the requirements of the law are written on their hearts, their consciences also bearing witness, and their thoughts now accusing, now even defending them.) [16]This will take place on the day when God will judge men's secrets through Jesus Christ, as my gospel declares.

That's a mouthful I know, so let's unpack it a bit so we can better understand what he is talking about. Stay with me now.

Notice in verse 16 that he starts out 'This will take place', which indicates that whatever is going to take place is what he describes in the verses above. So verse 16 is a key part of what he is saying.

Verses 13-15 have traditionally been rendered in parenthesis in English translations, though the NIV does not place verse 13 inside the parenthesis. This makes verses 13-15 a parenthetical statement (meaning it is an explanatory statement, like this) expanding on what was said in verse 12.

If you remove the parenthetical statement (verses 13-15), you are left with verses 12 and 16:

"All who sin apart from the law will also perish apart from the law, and all who sin under the law will be judged by the law... This will take place on the day when God will judge men's secrets through Jesus Christ, as my gospel declares."

Now it becomes clear that Paul is telling us part of what his gospel declares; that there will be a day when men will be judged by God, through Jesus Christ, according to the law.

In verse 13, he is saying that just because you have heard the law doesn't mean you have kept the law. It's almost like saying, "You Jews think that because you 'have' the law that you will be declared righteous, even though you haven't kept it."

In verses 14 and 15 he continues by saying, in effect, "Look at the gentiles. They keep some of the law by nature, though they do not 'have' the law, proving that the law is written on their hearts and consciences. Though they do not have the written code, they still know right from wrong."

No one is exempt from judgment according to the law because we all have it written on our hearts, and our consciences judge our actions against it.

Conscientious Appeal

While there are emotional and intellectual aspects to the gospel message, the primary appeal of the law is to the intellect through the conscience. As is clear from verses 14 and 15 of the passage above (Romans 2) the law of God is written on men's hearts. As they keep or violate that law, their consciences are continually defending or accusing them, respectively. The word conscience literally means 'with' (con) 'knowledge' (science). So when men violate the law of God that is in their hearts, they do it with knowledge that they are doing wrong.

The written law leads sinners to recognize their need for Christ by bringing them to an intellectual acknowledgement of accountability for sin before God. While we are aware that we have often violated our consciences, we can learn to ignore that. But when suddenly confronted with the commandments, a standard of God external to both the intellect and the conscience, the intellect concedes that the conscience has been right all along. In a sense, it is the mind saying "Aha! I knew because of the nagging of my conscience that I was doing wrong. I could ignore my conscience easily enough, but now I recognize that I am accountable not only to my conscience, but to God."

Once one begins to understand that there is a Holy God who

has issued a Holy law by which humanity will be judged, and that he has violated that law, the punishment of sin as lawlessness makes sense. It becomes intellectually reasonable that God is just in His condemnation of the sinner.

Judge Not

When we lead others to God's standard, we are not judging them. In John 3:17 Jesus said that God did not send his son into the world to judge the world, and neither are we to judge the world.

God is the one who will judge all men. Remember that whoever does not believe in the Son stands condemned already before God. It is not our job to condemn anyone, but to show them that they are already condemned. This is truly one of the greatest kindnesses you can show anyone. This is why Paul used the law in his gospel to the gentiles; it is the standard by which all men will be judged and the only true way to the knowledge of sin. The Ten Commandments are practice for judgment day, if you will.

One thing which *we* as Christians tend to judge (among many) is homosexuality. I have heard people say that when you witness to a homosexual, you should bring up their sexual perversion. When you use the law this becomes practically irrelevant. Revelation 21:8 says that the sexually immoral will have their part in the lake of fire, which is the second death. It also clearly states that all liars will have their part in the lake of fire. So if the person to whom you are witnessing has told one lie, he has broken the whole of God's law and is wholly condemned apart from his perversion. Badgering him about his personal sins will only lead to an argument.

Another wonderful thing about the Ten Commandments is that they are universal to all mankind. In the example above, we might be able to say that we have never been guilty of homosexual behavior and so by comparison are 'clean'. But God doesn't let us get away with that. He evens the playing field, naming sins that are common to all people so that no one can use His standard as proof that they are more righteous than anyone else, since we have all broken them at one time or another. Scripture tells us that if we have broken the least significant tenet of the law, we have broken the whole. Anyone who claimed that he had never broken any of the Commandments would have to be insane or lying. If he were lying, of course, he would be breaking the ninth, thereby disproving his case.

Paul gave Timothy some good advice in the book of 2 Timothy.

"Don't have anything to do with foolish and stupid arguments, because you know they produce quarrels.

And the Lord's servant must not quarrel; instead, he must be kind to everyone, able to teach, not resentful."[19]

Never, ever say anything out of resentment when presenting the gospel. Arguments are completely unproductive.

As he continues, he gives the best description of evangelism that can be found in scripture, and one that every person interested in evangelism should commit to memory;

"Those who oppose him he must gently instruct, in the hope that God will grant them repentance leading them to a knowledge of the truth, and that they will come to their senses and escape from the trap of the devil, who has taken them captive to do his will."[20]

This is what we are doing, really. We are gently instructing in the hope that God will lead to repentance.

In Galatians 3:24, where we learned that the law leads us to Christ, the phrase translated 'put in charge to lead' connotes a servant whose job was to lead children to school. When we are preaching, we should be ever aware that we are not judging, but teaching. We are leading the spiritually ignorant into God's classroom. We are no better than they, except that we've already been schooled. We are all sinners. We all sin. The moment we cross the line between showing someone that God will justly

[19] 2 TIMOTHY 2:23-24
[20] 2 TIMOTHY 2:25-26

judge them for sin and unjustly judging their sin ourselves, we are sinning. Legal use of the law will keep us honest by making us realize that without Christ we are no more righteous than anyone else.

Preaching Plagues

The real problem that man has with God is pride. We may be so full of pride that we refuse to acknowledge God, or in our pride we may even begin to think that we are doing right in the eyes of God by keeping the law. God through Isaiah the prophet rebuked the nation of Israel for this very sin:

"For my thoughts are not your thoughts,

neither are your ways my ways,"

declares the LORD.

"As the heavens are higher than the earth,

so are my ways higher than your ways

and my thoughts than your thoughts." [21]

We *think* we are wise. But wisdom only comes when we begin to fear the Lord and approach Him with humility[22], which is the true purpose of the law. After God had delivered the Ten Commandments in Exodus chapter 20, Moses said to the

[21] PROVERBS 26:12
[22] PROVERBS 1:7

people, "God has come to test you, that the fear of him may be before you, that you may not sin."[23] From the beginning, this law was a test revealing the nature of sin and leading God's people to a reliance on His mercy.

The law has the power to convince people of their sin, and before this holy law our attempts to justify our sin are revealed as ludicrous. Paul writes in Romans 3:19:

> "...whatever the law says, it says to those who are under the law, so that every mouth may be silenced and the whole world held accountable to God."

Though our consciences make us aware of our wrongdoing with feelings of guilt, The Bible tells us that our hearts are inherently wicked, leading us to continually try to justify our sin to ourselves, those around us, and God. The law of God has the effect of humbling the heart of man by making us realize that we are ultimately accountable not just to our conscience, but before God, which stops the mind and the mouth from justifying sin.

The history of the exodus of the Israelites from Egypt is a wonderful type of the use of the law in evangelism. They were in bondage to the Egyptians, just as humanity is enslaved to sin. God sent Moses to Pharaoh with the message that he should let

[23] EXODUS 20:20 (ESV)

the Israelites go, just as the evangelist appeals to the conscience of the sinner. Of course the Egyptians, like the kingdom of this world, were reluctant to release their slaves. So God sent ten plagues upon Pharaoh and the Egyptians, corresponding to the effect of the Ten Commandments upon the sin nature of a sinner. It is interesting to note Pharaoh's response as each of these plagues come to pass. It is astonishingly similar to the response of a sinner to hearing the commandments.

At the first plague, Pharaoh ignored God completely. He had his magicians turn the Nile to blood as Moses had done after the manner of one confronted with a Commandment who claims, "Big deal! Everyone has done that!"

Through several more, Pharaoh began to acknowledge God, but would not let Israel go. He even investigated the plagues to confirm that what Moses had told him was the truth, but his heart remained hard.

By the seventh, the plague of hail, Pharaoh acknowledges his sin:

"Then Pharaoh summoned Moses and Aaron. 'This time I have sinned,' he said to them. 'The LORD is in the right, and I and my people are in the wrong. Pray to the LORD, for we have had enough thunder and hail. I will let you go; you don't have to stay any longer.'"[24]

But still he would not let go of the Israelites. What a picture this is of the sinner grasping his sin! He will acknowledge that he has sinned, but will not turn from it.

At the eighth, the locusts, Pharaoh agrees to let the men go on the condition that they leave behind their women, children and livestock. He desperately wants to get Moses and his plagues out of his life, but only on his terms. The sinner comes to the place where he wants to bargain with God over which Commandments he will obey.

At the plague of darkness, number nine, Pharaoh agrees to let the women and children go so long as the livestock stay. He is giving in a little more at each plague, but has still not surrendered.

Finally we get to plague number ten, the death of every first-born Egyptian. This is too much for Pharaoh.

"During the night Pharaoh summoned Moses and Aaron and said, 'Up! Leave my people, you and the Israelites! Go, worship the LORD as you have requested. Take your flocks and herds, as you have said, and go.'"[25]

Just as Pharaoh had had all of the plagues he could stand, the

---

[24] EXODUS 9:27-28
[25] EXODUS 12:31-32

conscience of the sinner under the plagues of the commandments will eventually have to surrender or accept sure destruction. If he surrenders, the world must relinquish him to God.

All of this plaguing eventually culminates in the Passover, that most excellent Old Testament type of the sacrifice of Christ. This is the equivalent of the evangelist's preaching of grace following the law. The Israelites in Egypt were instructed to sacrifice a lamb and place the blood on their doorposts. Having done this, they waited in faith as the angel of death passed over the land, bringing death to every home which was not covered by the blood. The evangelist instructs the sinner to place faith in the blood sacrifice of Jesus Christ, and so to avoid the judgment of God. It was the plagues that proved God's earnest judgment and spurred the Israelites to obedience. Without them, the observance of the Passover would surely have seemed foolishness. In the same way, it is the Commandments that make the grace of God reasonable and attractive to the sinner and make 'the foolishness of what is preached' appealing.

After plaguing the sinner with the Commandments, he (or at least his sinful nature) should be where Pharaoh eventually ended up. His will to argue is gone. His mouth is silenced, just as Paul states in Romans 3:19. He begins to realize that he alone is accountable to God for his sin. It no longer matters that someone else has sinned worse than he has, for God cannot tolerate *any* sin. His mouth literally stops trying to justify his actions.

God always opposes the proud but gives grace to the humble.[26] Jesus gives us a word of warning regarding sharing grace with the arrogant – those who have not been brought to a point of desperation for God. In Matthew 7:6, he says:

"Do not give dogs what is sacred; do not throw your pearls to pigs. If you do, they may trample them under their feet, and then turn and tear you to pieces."

The greatest pearl we have is the gospel of Jesus Christ. Until someone's mouth has stopped and he has become accountable before God, do not give him that pearl unless you want him to trample it and tear you to pieces.

Here Comes the Judge

The Ten Commandments show a person his condemnation before God, but it must be equally understood that there is a coming judgment. Lawless acts will not merely slip away into oblivion, but will one day be confessed to and judged by God Almighty. In that day the unbeliever will have to admit his guilt before God, and it will be too late to seek the savior for pardon.

---

[26] PROVERBS 3:34

No person on earth today can say with certainty that he will be here tomorrow. The Bible makes it clear that "man is destined to die once, and after that to face the judgment."[27] At the judgment seat, the Commandments will be either our best friend or our worst enemy. None of us will be able to plead that we are not guilty of breaking them on that day, but to those who understood the legal use of the law and fled to the savior in this lifetime there will be pardon. For those who never did heed the law, or expected to be saved by keeping the law, it will stand in judgment over them and send them to eternal condemnation and torment.

Conclusion

God does not make mistakes. The old covenant was not a misconceived 'Plan A' with the new covenant saving the day. God put His law in place for a very specific reason; to show all the world what sin is. It is an unbending standard by which mankind will be judged. If we use it as Paul did in his ministry to the gentiles, then at the judgment seat those who have accepted the savior will have the utmost love and respect for that law which led them to the savior. If not, it will be too late for them by the time the books are opened and the law is read. That very law which God meant to lead them to His mercy will

---

[27] HEBREWS 9:27

condemn them to eternal torment. By painting an unbeliever into a corner, the law leaves them no option but to seek God for His grace or reject Him out rightly.

HOW SWEET THE SOUND

GOD MADE HIM WHO HAD NO SIN TO BE SIN FOR US, SO THAT IN HIM WE MIGHT BECOME THE RIGHTEOUSNESS OF GOD.

2 CORINTHIANS 5:21

The law creates in the heart of the sinner a desperate need for the mercy of God. This is the pattern for Christian faith – desperate need for God. Those who would place their faith in Jesus Christ need to know that they can never, ever please God by their works. It is the law that makes them realize this. If we present the gospel to them in a way that does not allow them to grasp their hopelessness, they will very likely enter into a relationship with God that is based on keeping the law and not on the mercy of God. Paul said, "For through the law I died to the law, so that I might live to God."[1] Those who are not dead to the law will remain in bondage to the law, trying to please God by what they do and not by humble dependence on His grace, as he intends.

---

[1] GALATIANS 2:19

If the law is used properly, however, the unbeliever will recognize the futility of trying to keep the law and the good news becomes exceedingly good. Listen to the words of John 3:16:

> "For God so loved the world that he gave his one and only Son, that whoever believes in him shall not perish but have eternal life."

How sweet the sound of this amazing grace to the humble heart!

The Value of Grace

I hear a lot of complaining against 'cheap grace' in the church today, and I often wonder if we understand what that even means. The same people that complain about it are pedaling a life-enhancement message. The gospel of The Bible really has very little to do with life enhancement, at least from the God's point of view. When we try and make it all about what God can do for us, no matter how subtly, we cheapen it severely.

The gospel is a message of self-denial and not self-improvement. Jesus plainly stated, "Whoever finds their life will lose it, and whoever loses their life for my sake will find it."[2] It is not a call to add something good to our lives or remove something bad from our lives, but to completely give our lives up for something of infinitely more worth than anything this

[2] MATTHEW 10:39

world can offer – the righteousness of God in Christ Jesus.

Listen to the language of Paul as he compares the grace of God with worldly gain:

> "But whatever gain I had, I counted as loss for the sake of Christ. Indeed, I count everything as loss because of the surpassing worth of knowing Christ Jesus my Lord. For his sake I have suffered the loss of all things and count them as rubbish, in order that I may gain Christ and be found in him, not having a righteousness of my own that comes from the law, but that which comes through faith in Christ…"[3]

We seldom preach a message of righteousness by faith that could allow someone to respond to the gospel in this manner. In fact, most of us probably don't even understand that the gospel is related specifically to this righteousness; it asks us to come and through faith partake of the righteousness of Christ so that we may have a relationship with God, and should also plainly state that there is nothing else we can do that will please God and turn away His just wrath toward us as sinners.

Without the righteousness by faith which is imputed to us when we hear and believe the gospel, there can be no relationship with God. Apart from Christ we have no basis on

[3] PHILIPPIANS 3:8-9 (ESV)

which to approach God and ask His forgiveness for our sins. We deserve nothing less than His wrath for our lawless deeds, and for Him to simply forgive us because we ask would be contrary to His nature as He is completely holy and just. This is why Christ had to die on the cross, as a payment for our sins[4]. It is by faith in that substitutionary atonement alone that we can have a relationship with God. Jesus procured our forgiveness with his blood, and until we can completely trust in him alone as payment for all of our sin, we cannot be forgiven our lawlessness or set free from the condemnation that the law brings.

What becomes of our lives should be an outgrowth of this righteousness we obtain in Christ. The fruit of a new life can only spring forth from this unmerited righteousness, so to tell someone that the purpose of the cross is to enhance their lifestyle is to lead them to expect a harvest of fruit from a tree whose seed has never been planted. They will eventually spiritually starve to death as they struggle to reap fruit year after year, futilely watering and fertilizing the ground with their own works in anticipation of the promised harvest.

As an example of the life enhancement message, here is an excerpt from a brochure given to those who attended a local crusade:

---

[4] ROMANS 3:21-26

Whatever situations or emotions you struggle with...
loneliness, guilt, stress, suicide, life after death, purpose in
life, drugs... **There is an Answer!** God loves you and
offers you His best.

We may see no problem with that message. As Christians,
many of us have experienced the power of God in our lives to
change our hearts and minds, and so we recognize the truth in
it. The problem with it is that it promises fruit without even
addressing the sinner's need for the *righteousness of God*. It takes
the glorious, miraculous grace of God and equates it to a rehab
program. To understand how amazing God's grace really is, we
need to abandon the idea that life enhancement is the aim of the
gospel.

Jesus died on the cross to take our punishment for sin and
make us righteous before God. He did not die to take away our
pain, trials or suffering. In fact, he promised that we would have
trouble in this life[5]. When we tell people that Jesus died to
enhance their life here on earth, we lead them into false hope
and teach them to drastically undervalue grace.

We may think that no one can be truly happy without Christ.
But there are many in the world who are perfectly happy with
their lives as they are. So man can, in his limited understanding,
be happy. There are programs in the world that are not Christ-

5 JOHN 16:33

based and yet are successful in breaking addictions. Whether we want to admit it or not, man can beat addiction. Man can make large strides toward curing mental illness, depression, and sickness. Men throughout the ages have found purpose in many pursuits. So, hard as it may be to accept, we do not absolutely require Christ to deal with any of our lifestyle issues. Many of these things can be overcome by force of human will.

There is one thing that man can *never, ever* overcome on his own, though; unrighteousness.

That is the amazing thing about grace; not its power to break addictions or the fact that it brings purpose to life, but that it declares us righteous before God despite our utter sinfulness. As we seek this righteousness in Christ, all of these other things fall into place.[6] Enhancement of our earthly life is a wonderful result of this righteousness, not the purpose for it.

When we try to sell the gospel as the answer for worldly sorrow, we are comparing apples and oranges. We can make people respond to our message for the wrong reasons. Paul said,

"Godly sorrow brings repentance that leads to salvation and leaves no regret, but worldly sorrow brings death."[7]

When our evangelistic message appeals to people's sense of worldly sorrow, we can inadvertently lead them to death. Our

[6] MATTHEW 6:33
[7] 2 CORINTHIANS 7:10

job is to bring them to the place of Godly sorrow that leads to repentance by the use of the law, as we saw in the last chapter.

Consider what could happen if we were to 'win' someone to Christ with the promise of an end to their worldly sorrow. We tell them, for example, that our God is big enough to overcome their drug addiction. What happens when that drug addiction is gone? What need do they now have for Christ in their lives? If we lead people into believing that God's purpose is to remove their worldly sorrow, they may understandably think that that is God's reason for being, completely missing the infinitely greater things that God has in store for them. We have introduced them to a god with a lowercase 'g'.

Your Own Personal Jesus

During the three years of Jesus' earthly ministry, he was surrounded by disciples. While these men admitted that they believed that he was the Messiah, they evidently did not yet believe in *him*. They believed in a concept of who Messiah should be, and they had faith in that concept, not the God-man Jesus.

They anticipated a conquering savior that would lead Israel to independence and prominence, not the suffering servant that had come to redeem mankind from sin. They missed the greater purpose of God because they had fixed their eyes and hearts on the temporal and not the eternal.[8] Even after his crucifixion and resurrection, they exhibited their ignorance of his true purpose when they asked, "Lord, are you at this time going to restore the kingdom to Israel?"[9] With the benefit of hindsight, we can see that despite the fact that they had witnessed the greatest intervention of God in history, they were still looking for him to fulfill their earthbound expectations.

They viewed him through the filter of their temporal desires, creating for themselves a kind personal Jesus that had no basis in eternal reality. Cheap grace, undervalued grace, a grace that is not rooted in the righteousness of Christ, can lead people into this same kind of personal expectation and inevitable disappointment.

One of the principal reasons that Paul preached the gospel so carefully was to avoid leading his hearers to this kind of vain belief.

> "By *this* gospel you are saved, if you hold firmly to the word I preached to you. Otherwise, you have believed in vain."[10]

When we preach a gospel that undervalues grace, we can entice people with a cheap grace to a cheap faith in a cheap savior.

[8] 2 CORINTHIANS 4:18
[9] ACTS 1:6
[10] 1 CORINTHIANS 15:2

Hear me - I am not saying that Jesus is cheap - I am saying that when we fail to preach the extravagant richness of God's righteousness and freedom through Jesus Christ, people will miss it and suffer for it. In a state of 'almost grace', many will unconsciously turn once again to the works of the law for justification, laboring for years to please a demanding and disappointing Jesus of their own understanding. As Martin Luther said "God is incomprehensible and invisible, therefore what may be seen and comprehended, that is not God." If we allow people to view God as a solution to temporal issues, they can easily miss the powerful, life-changing righteousness that is at the core of the gospel.

The Transaction

Since we are tasked with bringing people to knowledge of this glorious truth, we need to be able to relate grace in a way that they can understand. And in order to do that, we need to understand it thoroughly ourselves.

Grace is a legal transaction. I know that does not sound very romantic, nor does it make good hymn fodder, but it is the truth. Let's look at 2 Corinthians 5:21:

"God made him who had no sin to be sin for us, so that in him we might become the righteousness of God."

Jesus was perfectly sinless. The Bible says that he was tempted in every way, and yet remained without sin[11], and in order to atone for the sins of all mankind, he must be so. He had to live a life of perfect holiness that fulfilled the demands of the law. In a very real way, he lived in our place as much as he died in our place. Being sinless, he became a sin offering for us. He exchanged his life for ours, purchasing our pardon from God. When we recognize his sacrifice in our place, we "become the righteousness of God". Like Abraham, our faith alone is credited to us as righteousness.

This righteousness by faith is at the very heart of the biblical gospel – it is the goal of God's message to humankind, despite what we may think to the contrary. In essence, it states:

1. As demonstrated by our inability to keep God's law, no one is righteous, and He will justly judge the lawlessness of the unrighteous

2. No one can become righteous in God's sight by observance of the law

3. Jesus must, by faith, become our righteousness if we are to avoid judgment and be reconciled to God

The law creates a sin debt to God so deep that we can *never* repay it. Paul describes it like this in Colossians 2:

"And you, who were dead in your trespasses and the

---

[11] HEBREWS 4:15

uncircumcision of your flesh, God made alive together with him, having forgiven us all our trespasses, by canceling the record of debt that stood against us with its legal demands. This he set aside, nailing it to the cross."

The scope of this debt is so outside of our ability to pay that our best efforts are ridiculously, pathetically inadequate; yet this debt must be satisfied in order for us to be reconciled to God. The sinless Son of God is the only one who could ever adequately repay the debt - and has done so - so that when we recognize, by faith, his sacrifice as our payment we assume his righteousness as our own.

Jesus fulfilled the law by living a sinless life and satisfied the requirement for blood atonement[12] on the cross, completing a transaction with God for humankind. By his perfect life he fulfilled the requirements of and judgment by the law. Our debt has been completely paid, so God can legally dismiss our case on judgment day. We can live, speak and think boldly in the assurance of these things, even as Paul did, because they are the gospel truth.

Trusting the Savior

As I have stated elsewhere, the grace of God is not universal; in other words, it does not universally cleanse all mankind from

---

[12] HEBREWS 9:22

sin. We must accept the reality that we are covered by his sacrifice to benefit from it - but we are free to refuse it. Any person can willingly refuse the gospel and choose to go to hell.

When we use the phrase 'trust in the savior', it means just that. We must trust that the sacrifice of Christ alone makes us righteous before God. We can never again trust in our own goodness; we must by faith know that Christ is our only goodness. There is nothing, good or bad, that we can do to jeopardize our standing with God so long as we continue to trust him in this way.

We need to trust him in the way we trust the air that we breathe. Without having to think about the exact mix of gasses present in it, we instinctively know that it will sustain us with each breath. In the same way we must realize that our faith in Christ is the righteousness that sustains us before a holy God. We don't need to fully understand what that means, but we must know that it is true. Most importantly, we have to come to grips with the fact that we cannot create our own righteousness any more than we can create the air that we breathe. Knowing this inspires in us a desperate need to be where God is and remain in the atmosphere of Christ's righteousness for our own survival.

A sinner who comes to understand his hopeless state before God should literally claw his way to the savior as he would fight for air underwater. There is no need for 'every head bowed, every eye closed' when someone is moved by the call of God and recognizes that grace is the only thing standing between him and eternal damnation. At this point, finally, the love of God, expressed through the death of his son, makes sense to the sinner. And how sweet the sound of that amazing grace!

Repentance

It is interesting to me that we use the term 'decision for Christ' to describe conversion. First, it implies that we play a much larger role in salvation than I think scripture describes. Considering that God does pretty much all the work of salvation, our 'decision' is relatively trivial (albeit important). Secondly, when inspired by the conviction of the Holy Spirit, conversion, preceded by repentance, could not be described so much as a decision as a spiritual implosion. Recognizing that I am a sinful creature coming face-to-face with the Holy Creator, my response should be something more than, "Well, I've tried everything else. Let's give it a go."

The goal of the evangelist is not to get decisions. Our goal is repentance. This was the goal of Christ's ministry on earth:

"I have not come to call the righteous, but sinners to

repentance."[13]

At the beginning of his earthly ministry, Jesus began by proclaiming "Repent and believe the good news"[14], not one or the other, but both. John the Baptist instructed to "produce fruit in keeping with repentance."[15] Jesus talks about the joy that results in heaven when a sinner repents[16], but does not mention any heavenly response to decisions. Repentance is a necessary part of salvation; it is what God looks for, and so should we.

Repentance is a change of heart and mind. It means that where we have been lawbreakers in the past, we consciously choose to stop breaking God's law; not because we are going to try harder to keep the law, but because we have a new relationship to it. We will explore that topic in several more chapters.

Cancelling Fire Insurance

I hope to put an end to the idea that the biblical gospel is 'fire insurance'. If you have been able to follow the narrative of this book, you should have realized that, scripturally, there is one reason that the world has for turning to God; to save themselves from judgment because of their unrighteousness. We need to

[13] MATTHEW 5:32
[14] MARK 1:15
[15] MATTHEW 3:8
[16] LUKE 15:7

stop treating this truth as if it's a bad thing. The fact is that the more we sell the gospel as the answer to the problems of this life rather than the answer to unrighteousness that will lead to condemnation, the more we undervalue it in the eyes of a potential believer. As Paul said, "If only for this life we have hope in Christ, we are of all people most to be pitied."[17]

Scripture is clear enough about the mindset of the unbeliever to disabuse us of any notion that the love of God will attract people to salvation. If we tell people that God loves them just as they are, in their pride and sin, we are presuming upon God and lying to them. Psalm 5:4-6 says:

"You are not a God who takes pleasure in evil;

with you the wicked cannot dwell.

The arrogant cannot stand in your presence;

you hate all who do wrong.

You destroy those who tell lies;

bloodthirsty and deceitful men

the LORD abhors."

God will justly judge unrepentant sinners. He has called all people everywhere to repentance.[18] God's plan has always been,

[17] 1 CORINTHIANS 15:19
[18] ACTS 17:30

and always will be, to lead people to His mercy by the use of His law. It is a clear and conscious understanding of one's personal sin against God and the coming judgment that leads to repentance and reconciliation. God opposes the proud; any evangelical message that invites people to the cross while allowing their pride to remain intact may lead them into a religion of self-righteousness, but will almost certainly not lead them to Christ and salvation.

The gospel which was given to Paul has a built-in provision to defeat pride before an individual comes to the cross. The law creates in the hearer a fear of God that is absolutely healthy and necessary to his relationship with God. It allows the sinner to understand that God is righteously wrathful before he can understand that He is also incredibly merciful. It makes him realize his total reliance upon that mercy at the outset of his relationship with God, and through this process he is led to immense gratitude toward God. The biblical gospel is less 'fire insurance' than it is a 'smoke detector'. Its true purpose is to warn the sinner so that he may escape the flames; an escape so welcomed when it appears that it should create a deep and lasting appreciation of God's mercy.

While Jesus reclined at the table of Simon the Pharisee, a woman who had 'lived a sinful life' came and washed his feet with her tears, dried them with her hair, and anointed them with oil. Simon was appalled that Jesus would allow such a person to touch him. In response, Jesus related this parable:

> "Two people owed money to a certain moneylender. One owed him five hundred denarii and the other fifty. Neither of them had the money to pay him back, so he forgave the debts of both. Now which of them will love him more?"

> Simon replied, "I suppose the one who had the bigger debt forgiven."

> "You have judged correctly," Jesus said.[19]

The one who knew that he had been forgiven much loved much. The scriptural gospel allows a person to understand exactly what has been forgiven them and creates a love for God that can be fostered in no other way.

Conclusion

The message of the cross is wonderfully simple, but it makes sense only as we come to understand our need for it. Without an understanding of need, it is foolishness.

John Wesley once wrote, "Preach 90 percent Law and 10 percent grace." As unfamiliar as this may sound to us today, the reality is that if you preach the law correctly, you will never

[19] LUKE 7:41-43

need to spend more than about 10% of your time preaching grace. Once the Holy Spirit and the law have done their work in a prideful heart, this amazing grace will be quickly, humbly, and gratefully received by those who are called of God. They will be comforted.

THE COMFORTER

But you will receive power when the Holy Spirit comes on you; and you will be my witnesses in Jerusalem, and in all Judea and Samaria, and to the ends of the earth.

ACTS 1:8

Once a person understands that he is condemned before God, and has accepted the fact that God made a way for him to be declared righteous regardless of his sin, there should be a feeling of overwhelming gratitude in that person's heart. He will be grateful to God for forgiveness, grateful to Christ for his sacrifice, and grateful to the law for showing him the way to grace. This gratitude alone should lead to a desire for the things of God and holiness. But God does not leave us with just gratitude. He provides us with help to live a new life.

The Promise

Jesus did not just die on the cross to take the punishment for our sin; He rose from the dead so that we could, in him, live a life that is pleasing to God. This is another reason that God saves us; so that he might fulfill a promise:

"He redeemed us in order that the blessing given to Abraham [justification by faith] might come to the Gentiles through Christ Jesus, so that by faith we might receive the promise of the Spirit."[1]

Near the end of the last chapter, we talked about how Paul spoke of living in 'the new way of the Spirit', which superseded the old way of keeping the written code. The Jews had the law of the old covenant which was given to show them God's standard of righteousness. Jesus fulfilled that law by living a sinless life, dying upon the cross and rising from the dead, establishing a new covenant. So what governs the life of a new covenant believer?

God prophesied through Jeremiah that a time would come when the written law would be superseded by a new covenant:

"This is the covenant I will make with the house of Israel

after that time," declares the LORD.

"I will put my law in their minds

and write it on their hearts.

I will be their God,

and they will be my people."[2]

[1] GALATIANS 3:14
[2] JEREMIAH 31:33

Paul refers to this new law as 'the law of the Spirit of life' in Romans chapter 8. James calls it "the perfect law, the law of liberty..."[3] When we live by faith in what Christ has accomplished, we are given a new nature along with the Spirit. So, rather than trying to become something that we are not (as would be the case were we trying to keep the law) we become an entirely new creation with a new nature[4]. The Spirit brings about growth by making us increasingly what we already are – the righteousness of God in Christ.[5]

The Purpose

The work of the Holy Spirit has a wonderful effect in the life of the believer. He gives us power to grow in grace and the power to understand spiritual truth. But we need to understand that God did not give this gift just for our own betterment. He betters us through the Holy Spirit so that we may serve his purposes with our new lives.

We have a fantastic clue as to why we receive the Spirit in the promise that Jesus made to his disciples at his ascension:

"But you will receive power when the Holy Spirit comes on you; and you will be my witnesses in Jerusalem, and in

[3] JAMES 1:25
[4] 2 CORINTHIANS 5:17
[5] 2 CORINTHIANS 5:21

all Judea and Samaria, and to the ends of the earth."[6]

The power, abilities and gifts that we receive as a result of the indwelling of the Spirit do not have our improvement as an end. They improve us so that we may live lives that glorify God for the purpose of witnessing to the world.

As Jeremiah prophesied, God creates in us a new set of desires when he gives us the Spirit. He becomes our God and we become His people. If He dwells in us, our minds should no longer be absorbed by the things of this world.

"Those who live according to the sinful nature have their minds set on what that nature desires; but those who live in accordance with the Spirit have their minds set on what the Spirit desires."[7]

We should be absorbed in the furtherance of God's kingdom through everything we do, as this is the desire of the Spirit.

This is a good test to see where we stand with God. What are our minds set on? Are we more concerned with our homes, marriages, families, jobs, entertainment or hobbies than we are with the Kingdom of God?[8] Are we preoccupied with the temporal things of this world or the eternal things of God?[9] These are important questions. Jesus said "No one who puts his

[6] ACTS 1:8
[7] ROMANS 8:5
[8] LUKE 18:29
[9] 2 CORINTHIANS 4:18

hand to the plow and looks back is fit for service in the kingdom of God."[10] Since God gives us the Spirit to make us fit for service, what does it mean if we are looking back to the world? Paul adds this:

"You, however, are controlled not by the sinful nature but by the Spirit, if the Spirit of God lives in you. And if anyone does not have the Spirit of Christ, he does not belong to Christ."[11]

If we are not fulfilling the calling of God because we have no desire to fulfill it, we may not have the Holy Spirit dwelling within us. If we do not have the Spirit, we do not belong to Christ. If we do not belong to Christ, we are not saved. If you have little desire for the things of God, I suggest that you review the past several chapters and test yourself with the law of God. Maybe you have never been led to Christ by the law so that you may be justified by faith.

The Power

Jesus told the Jews who believed him, "If you hold to my teaching, you are really my disciples."[12] Holding to something indicates that we have grasped it to begin with. Many think that we have a discipleship crisis in the American church today –

[10] LUKE 9:62
[11] ROMANS 8:9
[12] JOHN 8:31

that we have done a poor job of teaching converts. In truth the problem might actually be that we have done too good a job of teaching the unconverted. The prevalence of apathy in the church toward the word of God, fellowship and prayer leads me to believe that our churches are actually packed with unbelievers. They are not really disciples because they have never been given the kind of teaching that they can hold to. There is no hunger or thirst for God's righteousness because the appetite for these things has never been whetted by the knowledge of God's saving power.

You cannot disciple an unregenerate person; the unspiritual mind will never grasp spiritual truth. At best you can create a religion of self-righteousness by teaching religious dogma, but you cannot teach the saving knowledge of Christ. Jesus, quoting the prophet Isaiah, said of the religious unbelievers of his day, "You will be ever hearing but never understanding; you will be ever seeing but never perceiving."[13] This is a perfect description of many in our churches today. Salvation is the foundation of discipleship; without true saving knowledge of Jesus Christ, which cannot be taught, you cannot be a disciple. Trying to disciple an unbeliever is literally like whipping a dead horse.

When we look at the church today, we often wonder what has happened to it and how it has become so much like the

13 MATTHEW 13:14

world. I firmly believe it is because so many have made 'decisions for Christ' without experiencing the liberating power of the grace of God which lies in the gospel truth. They have had a religious experience without ever having been saved. We teach and teach and teach and they are ever hearing and seeing without ever understanding or perceiving. Paul foresaw the state of the church today when he wrote to Timothy:

> "But mark this: There will be terrible times in the last days. People will be lovers of themselves, lovers of money, boastful, proud, abusive, disobedient to their parents, ungrateful, unholy, without love, unforgiving, slanderous, without self-control, brutal, not lovers of the good, treacherous, rash, conceited, lovers of pleasure rather than lovers of God — having a form of godliness but denying its power."[14]

It is apparent that he is writing about the church here because it would make no sense to point these things out otherwise[15]. Paul would not be surprised to see the unbelieving acting in this way. It is also apparent that it is not a lack of teaching that leads the church to this state; for he goes on to tell Timothy that people who behave in this way are "always learning but never able to acknowledge the truth."[16] He is describing a church that

---

[14] 2 TIMOTHY 3:1-4
[15] SEE 1 CORINTHIANS 5:9-13
[16] 2 TIMOTHY 3:7

refuses to acknowledge God's power, even as we so often do. Rather than perpetuating religious training, which fosters a form of godliness, we need to rely on the gospel and expect miraculous salvation and sanctification as the early church did.

The early church had no membership rolls or decision cards so far as I can tell. They were recognized as believers by the power of the Holy Spirit which was exhibited in their lives. It is interesting to note that while in modern times we are absorbed with judging the outside world the early church leaders, as evidenced by their writings, judged those in the church. They understood that unbelievers were unbelievers – no surprise there. The concern was for those who claimed to be believers without producing any evidence to back up that claim. If you were indeed a disciple, it showed. If not, you were suspect.

Will the Real Disciples Please Stand Up?

How could the 21st century discipleship model have worked in the early church? We say the ideal discipleship ratio is one teacher to one disciple, with one to twelve being about the maximum (based on the twelve disciples of the gospels). On the day of Pentecost there were 120 Disciples gathered in the upper room when the Holy Spirit descended upon them. Peter began preaching to those gathered in Jerusalem, and within hours about 3,000 people were saved![17] When you do the math, this would make each of the original 120 disciples, newly inhabited by the Spirit themselves, responsible to disciple 25 others. Within a few days, more than 5,000 would be added, making each responsible to disciple at least 70 others!

It is intriguing to me that Luke described these 3,000 as having been 'added to the church', not simply making decisions. In the modern church, we have come to expect that about 90% of those responding to a mass invitation will fall away. In other words, by modern standards, of the 3,000 that responded to Peter's message that day, we would expect 2,700 to walk away from their decision to follow Christ. Apparently there was a zero percent fall away rate in this case. We know what became of these converts, because we read in the following verse:

"They devoted themselves to the apostles' teaching and to the fellowship, to the breaking of bread and to prayer."[18]

Evidently they somehow understood what it meant to be disciples right from the start. How could that be without intensive follow-up and discipleship programs?

The answer seems to lie in the response of the people to the message that Peter preached that day. Scripture says that those who heard were "cut to the heart and said to Peter and the other

[17] ACTS 2:41
[18] ACTS 2:42

apostles, 'Brothers, what shall we do?'"[19] This was not 'heads bowed, eyes closed' evangelism; these people had clearly recognized that they were in desperate need of God's mercy. Peter preached without compromise in the expectation that the power of God would save people. When people are genuinely saved and the Spirit dwells within them, they are hungry for the things of God and will desire learning, fellowship and prayer. They will devote themselves to these things. Is that not discipleship?

The word 'disciple' does not appear in the New Testament after the Book of Acts. In the epistles, salvation and discipleship are spoken of synonymously. This makes sense when you consider that after the resurrection and ascension of Christ, the Holy Spirit was sent to disciple those who believe. The words of Jesus bear this out:

> "But the Counselor, the Holy Spirit, whom the Father will send in my name, will teach you all things and will remind you of everything I have said to you."[20]

During his earthly ministry, Jesus was discipling people who were yet to be saved and receive the Spirit. After the Spirit came, things changed drastically in the church, with the Spirit becoming the primary teacher, counselor and comforter. John

---

[19] ACTS 2:37
[20] JOHN 14:26

wrote in 1 John:

> "But the anointing that you received from him abides in
> you, and you have no need that anyone should teach you.
> But as his anointing teaches you about everything, and is
> true, and is no lie—just as it has taught you, abide in
> him."[21]

We can teach people of God, but only God can teach people
about himself. We are biographers, teaching what we know
from experience and our own understanding of the scripture,
but only God can teach them His very thoughts. Paul said,

> "The Spirit searches all things, even the deep things of
> God. For who knows a person's thoughts except their
> own spirit within them? In the same way no one knows
> the thoughts of God except the Spirit of God. What we
> have received is not the spirit of the world, but the Spirit
> who is from God, so that we may understand what God
> has freely given us."[22]

It is the Spirit who brings knowledge of who God is and what
He has given. It is not our place to tell a person that they have
assurance of salvation. If they are saved, the Holy Spirit will tell
them so. We need to exercise caution to prevent new believers
from becoming followers of us rather than Christ. We cannot

[21] 1 JOHN 2:27 ESV
[22] 1 CORINTHIANS 2:10-12

make anyone a follower of Christ any more than we can grant them salvation. We can only speak the truth in love and leave the results to God. In a word, we need to trust that God will make them followers of himself, as He has promised.

In no way does this mean that we should abandon the teaching of new believers. The word disciple means, literally, a learner or pupil. We must teach new believers from the scripture so that they can have an understanding of the greater mysteries of God; the deeper truths of scripture. But this should be something that they eagerly desire so that learning, rather than being solely an inculcation of religious principles, becomes a lifelong passionate search for divine truth. Learning the things of God should be something they devote themselves to with sincerity, not religious obligation. This kind of devotion can only come as we are diligent to accurately share the first and most important revelation that any believer encounters, the gospel of Jesus Christ.

I know that what I am suggesting here is radical. I can imagine that some are thinking I only want to get out of having to disciple people, and I do. In place of all the emphasis on discipleship in the church, I would rather we expend our energies teaching and preaching the gospel in the power of the Spirit with the expectation that God saves and the Spirit creates disciples. This is difficult for us to embrace because we cannot build a program that manifests the power of God to radically change lives, and we don't know how to communicate truth that cannot be packaged in practical terms. We prefer to keep on pretending that the Spirit is behind our 'relatable' teaching because it keeps us in an earthly realm where we can produce documented (though worldly) results. Unfortunately, it also keeps us from entering the realm of eternal truth where the power of God that actually changes hearts and lives resides.

The fact is that we have no control over the saving power of God, but if we could begin to preach a scriptural gospel in the power of the Spirit we might once again see that power unleashed to revive the modern church as it once built the early church. The most important thing we could possibly teach in our churches today is how to preach the biblical gospel clearly and accurately. There can be no other answer to the apathy of the church than the true saving and keeping power of God, which brings us full circle to Acts 1:8 wherein Jesus promised to send the Spirit to make us powerful witnesses in the world. We have tried virtually everything else to build the Kingdom without success, and until the day that we welcome the power of God in the gospel as a reality again, Christianity will continue to struggle as mere religion. The gospel has been, from the beginning, the antithesis of religion, not an entrance into it.

Conclusion

Please don't get the idea that I think any of this is easy to accept. I know it isn't. I can almost guarantee that as you have read these things you thought; that's all well and good, but it's impossible!

In a sense you are correct. The kingdom of God is impossible. The teachings are humanly incomprehensible. There is an expectation of complete reliance on God to which our human nature is hostile. There is absolutely nothing at all practical or conventional about any of it. Our part in all of it seems very inconsequential, and that does not satisfy our desire to take credit for our works. No matter how well we understand grace there is a part of us that wants to *earn* our salvation. That is of our flesh.

I would also imagine that, like me, there is a part of you that not only wants to believe it, but does believe it. There is that part of you that knows that the scripture is true without question, even though it often does not seem to make sense. Listen to that part. That is the wisdom of God that "calls things that are not as though they were."[23] That is the Comforter speaking.

[23] ROMANS 4:17

REVISITING LAW: THE POWER OF SIN

THE STING OF DEATH IS SIN, AND THE POWER OF SIN IS THE LAW. BUT THANKS BE TO GOD, WHO GIVES US THE VICTORY THROUGH OUR LORD JESUS CHRIST.

1 CORINTHIANS 15:56-57

So now that we have inherited God's righteousness through faith in the completed work of Christ and are indwelt by the Holy Spirit, are we done with sin? The answer is yes and no. In truth, sin is alive and well within our flesh and always will be until we are no longer in this flesh, but we have a choice of whether or not to feed it.

The Law of Sin and Death

Paul discovered an odd truth about sin; it feeds on the law. The choice we will have to make every day for the rest of our lives is not "will I sin or not?" but "will I walk in grace or under law?" Am I "the new man" or "the old man", as Paul would say? This is a critical decision because it will determine our relationship to sin and to God. In Romans chapter 7, Paul explains that "apart from the law, sin lies dead."[1] He then goes on to explain the correlation between sin and law in the life of a believer.

First, as Paul did, we must dispense with any notion that the law is sin. The law is holy and the commandment is holy, righteous and good[2].

"What then shall we say? That the law is sin? By no means!"[3]

What Paul discovered was not that the law itself was sin, but that when we try to keep the law the sin within our flesh seizes the opportunity to do good which is afforded by the law, and creates in us the desire to do exactly the opposite. Though we acknowledge with our minds that the law is right, we cannot carry it out because the sin within us wages war against our minds and causes us to break the very law we are trying to keep. In Romans 8:2, Paul labels this principal as 'the law of sin and death'. This spiritual principle is every bit as binding as any physical principal, such as the laws of gravity or inertia. Just as I always expect a heavy object to fall downward and not upward, I should expect that any attempt I make to try to please God by

[1] ROMANS 7:8 ESV
[2] ROMANS 7:12 ESV
[3] ROMANS 7:7 ESV

my performance will fail because "when I want to do right, evil lies close at hand."[4]

"The very commandment that promised life proved to be death to me. For sin, seizing an opportunity through the commandment, deceived me and through it killed me."[5]

What this means is that we cannot defeat sin by our own efforts, or even 'with God's help'. If you search the New Testament, you will find that while we are told to flee sin and to count ourselves dead to sin, we are never told to fight it. Jesus said, "And if your hand or your foot causes you to sin, cut it off and throw it away."[6] He does not say "Train your hand or foot not to sin." Why? Because, as Paul discovered, we can't fight sin. The good news is that we don't have to. Paul makes this clear in Romans 8:3-4:

"For God has done what the law, weakened by the flesh, could not do. By sending his own Son in the likeness of sinful flesh and for sin, he condemned sin in the flesh, in order that the righteous requirement of the law might be fulfilled in us, who walk not according to the flesh but according to the Spirit."

[4] ROMANS 7:21 ESV
[5] ROMANS 7:10-11 ESV
[6] MATTHEW 18:8 ESV

Skipping a Step

By trying to face the sin in our flesh head on, we are skipping a step. While it seems intuitive that a Christian indwelt by the Spirit should have the willpower to keep the law and please God, we cannot precisely *because* of the law of sin and death. The answer, once again, lies not with us but with the atoning work of Christ.

This is a familiar scripture passage that is frequently misinterpreted:

> "For freedom Christ has set us free; stand firm therefore,
> and do not submit again to a yoke of slavery."[7]

We often assume that Paul is telling us that Christ has freed us from the yoke of sin, and that we should refuse to fall back into it. But it is not sin that Paul is speaking of. It is the law. As he continues, he has strong words for the Galatian churches:

> "You are severed from Christ, you who would be justified
> by the law; you have fallen away from grace."[8]

The churches had come under the teaching of those who demanded that believers must be circumcised. To submit to circumcision, Paul insisted, was to be severed from the Savior and placed under obligation to keep the whole of the law. As

[7] GALATIANS 5:1 ESV
[8] GALATIANS 5:4 ESV

with unbelievers, the instant we try by the flesh to keep any part of the law as a means of pleasing God, we bring ourselves under obligation to all of it. Many will argue that Paul was speaking only of the ceremonial law (including circumcision and the sacrifice of animals for sin atonement) but in Romans 7 the law he uses to illustrate his principle of 'the law of sin and death' is the tenth Commandment, part of the moral law.

Here is the choice we have to make:

"But I say, walk by the Spirit, and you will not gratify the desires of the flesh. For the desires of the flesh are against the Spirit, and the desires of the Spirit are against the flesh, for these are opposed to each other, to keep you from doing the things you want to do. *But if you are led by the Spirit, you are not under the law.*"[9]

The last verse seems oddly placed, but with it Paul equates living under the law with walking in the flesh. The 'flesh' is that which is of human origin, that which we do by our own power. When we try, under our own power, to satisfy God by what we do (or don't do) we come back under the law of sin and death. Regardless of our intention to do right, this amounts to self-righteousness, the very thing which Jesus detested in the Pharisees. When we do this we are in effect saying that Christ *is not* sufficient. We treat Christ's righteousness as if it were

[9] GALATIANS 5:16-18 ESV

worthless when we try to create our own righteousness.

The only appeal the law can make is to our sense of self-righteousness; our innate desire to prove ourselves righteous before God and man. To walk under the law is to walk in the flesh. Just as the fruit of walking in the Spirit is love, joy, peace, patience, kindness, goodness, faithfulness, gentleness and self-control, the flesh attempting to satisfy the law produces its own kind of works; sexual immorality, impurity, sensuality, idolatry, sorcery and so forth.[10]

Self-righteousness is the underlying 'disease' that manifests itself in myriad sinful symptoms. Addictions to wealth, sex, power, work, possessions, and human approval (co-dependency) are actually an outgrowth of the self-righteousness of a heart that does not trust the sufficiency of Christ as expressed in the scriptural gospel. These are signs that deep inside we are still struggling to 'get' something we don't have, not walking in the all-encompassing grace that we already have. Ignorant of, disregarding or unwilling to submit to the righteousness that is already ours in Christ, we re-double our efforts to establish our own righteousness, which brings us under deeper subjection to the law of sin and death. This creates the vicious, confusing and frustrating cycle which Paul describes perfectly in the latter part of Romans 7.

[10] GALATIANS 5:19-23

The End of the Law for Righteousness

There is a particular and peculiar way in which Christ
defeated the power of sin on the cross. He completely fulfilled
the law so that we don't have to:

> "Do not think that I have come to abolish the Law or the
> Prophets; I have not come to abolish them but to fulfill
> them."[11]

It is important to note that the law was not abolished but
fulfilled at the cross. The law still has work to do in convicting
the unsaved and expressing the moral will of God, but once it
has driven us to Christ it cannot work righteousness in us and
need not as Christ has already done so. As believers, we need to
recognize the foolishness of trying to keep the law as a means of
establishing righteousness before God, for to do so leads to self-
righteousness and then sin as Paul explains in Romans 7. Look
at the following passages:

> "For Christ is the end of the law for righteousness to
> everyone who believes."[12]

> "Christ redeemed us from the curse of the law by
> becoming a curse for us—for it is written, 'Cursed is

---

[11] MATTHEW 5:17 ESV
[12] ROMANS 10:4 ESV

everyone who is hanged on a tree'..."[13]

"Likewise, my brothers, you also have died to the law through the body of Christ, so that you may belong to another, to him who has been raised from the dead, in order that we may bear fruit for God."[14]

You might be recognizing a pattern here. Paul says that apart from the law, sin lies dead. The gospel tells us that Christ defeated sin in a very counter-intuitive manner; he fulfilled the law by his perfect life and death so that when we identify ourselves with him we also die to the law, setting us 'apart from the law' so that 'sin lies dead'. Paul describes this process with clarity in Colossians 2:13-14 (ESV):

"And you, who were dead in your trespasses and the uncircumcision of your flesh, God made alive together with him, having forgiven us all our trespasses, *by canceling the record of debt that stood against us with its legal demands.* This he set aside, nailing it to the cross."

In effect, when we walk by faith in the righteousness of Christ and not by trying to observe the law, sin is deprived of its power and starves to death. If we set our minds on fulfilling the law by the flesh, sin will grow stronger in us day by day. As he expounds the law of sin and death in Romans 8, Paul states:

[13]GALATIANS 3:13 ESV
[14]ROMANS 7:4 ESV

"For to set the mind on the flesh is death, but to set the mind on the Spirit is life and peace. For the mind that is set on the flesh is hostile to God, for it does not submit to God's law; indeed, it cannot. Those who are in the flesh cannot please God."

He makes no distinction here between believer and unbeliever, only what the mind is set on. We all have essentially the same choice to make; will I try to please God by my performance of the law (which Paul says is impossible) or will I accept, by faith, the fact that Christ has fulfilled the law on my behalf and receive life and peace? Will I be a Romans 7 or a Romans 8 Christian? These are the wide and narrow gates that Jesus spoke of.

Ironically, we accept the fact that we need the grace of God to be saved when we realize that we can't keep the law, and then after we're saved we begin to try to please God by struggling to keep the law. Jesus kept the law for us, which means that the law is fulfilled in us only as, by faith, we receive what he has done on our behalf on a moment by moment basis. We need the gospel as a constant reminder of who we have become so that we continually recognize the futility of establishing our own identity apart from Christ. This alone can keep the monster of self-righteousness at bay.

We will readily believe that Jesus defeated death and sin on the cross, but shy away from his fulfillment of the law. We are, by nature, creatures which gravitate toward legalism. We want everything in a box; to know where our boundaries are because we expect to be rewarded or punished based on how well we stay within bounds. Grace demolishes that box. It says that we are not graded based on performance, but on relationship, free and unmerited. Grace is absolutely uncharted territory for us, so wild and undomesticated and counter-self that we are terrified of it! It truly frees us from the law of sin and death so that we might begin to fulfill the law in the new way of the Spirit.[15]

The Law of the Spirit of Life

Paul instructed the Colossians:

"Therefore, as you received Christ Jesus the Lord, so walk in him, rooted and built up in him and established in the faith, just as you were taught, abounding in thanksgiving."[16]

How did we receive Christ? By hearing and believing the gospel. How then ought we to walk in Christ? By hearing and believing the gospel.

Walking in the Spirit, keeping the law of the Spirit of life, consists of constantly bringing into remembrance the truth of

[15] ROMANS 7:6
[16] COLOSSIANS 2:6-7

the gospel. We need to understand as completely as we can the depth and the breadth of what Christ *has already* secured for us. It means an end to trying to perform well enough to garner God's blessing or avoid his punishment by recognizing that Christ's performance on our behalf *has* pleased God. In the first chapter of this epistle, Paul tells the Colossians what it is that they walk in:

> "May you be strengthened with all power, according to his glorious might, for all endurance and patience with joy, giving thanks to the Father, who *has qualified you* to share in the inheritance of the saints in light. *He has delivered us* from the domain of darkness and *transferred us* to the kingdom of his beloved Son, in *whom we have redemption*, the *forgiveness of sins*."[17]

There is no need to strive to qualify ourselves before God. Christ has qualified us. There is no need to struggle free of darkness. Christ has delivered us and transferred us to his kingdom. There is no need to try and redeem ourselves by our own works. Christ has redeemed us. There is no need for condemnation or shame. We are forgiven.

We have to make a choice daily whether we walk in all of this, which has already been accomplished, or whether we seek by the flesh to please God. When we focus on the box – rules,

[17] COLOSSIANS 1:11-14

laws, principles and regulations – we lose sight of the truth that we are absolutely, positively, unashamedly, unreservedly free to draw close to and please God by faith in what Jesus Christ alone has accomplished. This, also, is the gospel truth.

None of us expects that by our own force of will we can achieve eternal life; that we can defeat death. None of us expects to be able to defeat sin by our own willpower, though we try without even realizing it. But many (if not most) of us expect that we can and assume that we must try to keep the law, which is the very power of the sin that we struggle against. These three things are actually interrelated in a domino-like fashion, death is dependent on sin, and sin is dependent on the law:

"The sting of death is sin, and the power of sin is the law. But thanks be to God, who gives us the victory through our Lord Jesus Christ."[18]

Apart from the law, the power of sin is gone; apart from sin, the sting of death is gone. In a very real way, our redemption from sin and our victory over death are largely accomplished by Christ's fulfillment of the law. When you dismiss the truth that the law was fulfilled for the believer at the cross, you have a very difficult time reconciling the other two.

[18] 1 CORINTHIANS 15:56-57 ESV

Conclusion

Scripture shows us that to keep the law by our own righteousness is impossible. The biblical answer to sin is to trust in the completed work of Jesus Christ and stand firm against the temptation to walk in your own righteousness, the worst of all sins. As we do this, we will begin to realize something really wonderful about the gospel; it is not just the door to Christian life, it is life itself.

THE THRESHOLD

WHATEVER HAPPENS, CONDUCT YOURSELVES IN A MANNER WORTHY OF
THE GOSPEL OF CHRIST.

PHILIPPIANS 1:27

From one minute to the next, how do you know of God's love for you? Is it His blessing that shows you His love? Is it Holy Ghost goose bumps you feel during a worship service? Is it a sense of peace that you have deep down in your being?

It is all of these, at times. But God wants us to know, as believers, that he has loved us and does love us infinitely, and he wants us to know it every minute of every day.

He wants us to know it in hard times and good. When things are going our way and when they are not. When we have peace in our hearts and when we are frantic beyond reason. In all of this, God wants us to know exactly how much He loves us, whether we feel it or not. This is another purpose of the gospel.

Proof of God's Love

Scripture tells us again and again how much He loves us. In

the New Testament, the love of God is most often expressed through the message of the cross:

> "For God so loved the world that he gave his one and only Son, that whoever believes in him shall not perish but have eternal life."[1]

> "But God demonstrates his own love for us in this: While we were still sinners, Christ died for us."[2]

> "I have been crucified with Christ and I no longer live, but Christ lives in me. The life I live in the body, I live by faith in the Son of God, who loved me and gave himself for me."[3]

God's love is not something we have to feel to know. God's love is a fact. It was proven over two thousand years ago. When we start to think that we are unlovable, that we have let God down so badly that there is no way He can love us that is our flesh speaking to us. If we are trusting in Christ for our righteousness, God's love is not conditional. If you want to know how much He loves you, look to Calvary. See the blood as it spreads into the grain of the heavy timbers and soaks into the parched earth of Golgotha. Smell the gall. Hear the wailing.

This is proof of God's love.

[1] JOHN 3:16
[2] ROMANS 5:8
[3] GALATIANS 2:20

In the moment that Jesus breathed his last, everything changed. Nothing would ever be the same again. The world was to be forever changed by that one act of obedience, and there was never to be any question as to whether God loved humankind again. It was finished and remains so to this day.

This is the very heart of the gospel. In dying, Jesus took all of the sin of humankind upon himself. The punishment that humanity has merited by our lawlessness toward God was placed upon him. As the wrath of a just and jealous God rained down upon the sinless Son of God, a door was opened between heaven and earth. The law can no longer hold sway over those who believe. And if we believe, we have discovered that door.

The Threshold

Think of that door as the gospel. At some point in time, all of us who are now believers were told of the door by someone, and God opened our eyes so that we were able to see it. And most of us think that we merely walked through it at that point, and it had done its work. The gospel had done its work. We were saved and on to bigger and better things.

But what if the door is not something you just walk through on the way to someplace else? What if we never really walked through it at all, but stepped just onto the threshold? If we look one way, we can still see the world. If we turn and look the other, we can see God. All we perceive of God is what we see framed by the door. All we perceive of the world is what we see framed by the same door.

In this way, the gospel becomes our link to both God and the world. When we look out on the world, we view it through the gospel. When we look to God, we view Him through the gospel as well. Our relationship to the world takes place from the threshold of the door, as does our relationship to God. Everything in life is funneled through the narrow door of the cross of Christ. If we begin to look at the gospel as something we never leave behind, as something that is always with us, shaping all of our perceptions of God and the world, it takes on a new life. It becomes life itself.

In Ephesians 6, Paul talks about the armor of God. He instructs us to "put on the full armor of God, so that when the day of evil comes, you may be able to stand your ground, and after you have done everything, to stand."[4] When we have fought until we can't fight anymore, we are instructed to stand and stand firm.

Among all the battle dress of a Roman soldier, Paul equates the gospel to shoes; "…with your feet fitted with the readiness that comes from the gospel of peace."[5] Most often we have

---

[4] EPHESIANS 6:13
[5] EPHESIANS 6:15

taught that the feet are fitted with the gospel in the sense that they move us about so that we might take the gospel to the world. But what if Paul is really saying that the gospel is what we must stand on? A foot soldier, above all things, must be sure footed. He must be able to move quickly. It would never do to dress in full battle armor and go onto the field of battle barefooted. No army could charge an enemy while being halted by each pebble and stone in their path. A soldier needs a foundation on which to stand, so that even after he has fought until he can fight no more, he still stands firm. The gospel is that which makes our advance into enemy territory possible; it keeps us from stumbling over the pebbles of this world.

Notice that our feet are to be 'fitted with the readiness that comes from the gospel'; meaning that wherever we go that readiness goes with us. This is contrary to our usual way of thinking of the gospel as something we heard and believed and moved past. Indeed, if we moved past it, then we are no longer ready for battle.

Carrying His Death

Sometimes I think that we get the idea that we left the gospel outside when we entered the door of the church. If so, we are mistaken. If we were truly saved, it is the law that we left behind. Paul says, "For through the law I died to the law so that

I might live for God."[6] D.L. Moody put it quite nicely when he said "The law can only chase a man to Calvary, no further." The law we leave behind after it has done its work, but the gospel must ever be with us. In order that the resurrected life of Jesus may be revealed in our bodies, we must always carry his death around in our bodies[7] in the acknowledgement of his sacrifice for us.

Without that continually open door, our approach to God is walled off. If we want to be where God is, we have to stay in the door. When we pray, we pray through the door. When we receive blessing, knowledge and insight, we receive it through the door. When we speak to the world, we speak through the door. All of Christian life is founded in the gospel. Everything we receive, everything we give. Jesus is our intercessor before God, and our only link to him this side of heaven is the gospel – that which we have heard and believed. It is the touchstone of our faith – "faith comes from hearing the message, and the message is heard through the word of Christ."[8] Every thought, every decision, every action should be weighed in light of that truth.

The gospel has too long been thought of as a tool of the evangelist when in reality it is the basis for our life, faith and

[6] GALATIANS 2:19
[7] 2 CORINTHIANS 4:10
[8] ROMANS 10:17

confidence in God. By basis I mean both the beginning and the foundation. Through the biblical gospel we know our God – His love, His mercy, His justice, His wrath. Every attribute of God is revealed in the biblical gospel. Not only does it introduce us to God personally, it continues to be the way of access to God. Apart from our understanding and acceptance of the redeeming work of Jesus Christ, there can be no relationship with God. This is true of believers and unbelievers alike. If by saying, "I am saved" you mean you responded to an alter call once, but the gospel is not as fresh and fascinating and challenging today as it ever was to you, then you are probably not in fellowship with God. You have stepped off of the threshold.

Equally it teaches us about our world. By it is the constantly expanding knowledge of God's grace that "teaches us to say 'No' to ungodliness and worldly passions, and to live self-controlled, upright and godly lives in this present age..."[9] When we think we have moved past it, we are kidding ourselves. We are walking into battle without shoes on. Framed by the doorpost of heaven it is impossible to fall in love with the things of this world. We can see them for what they are; temporary and worthless compared to what God has for us.

Believing the gospel, as stated before, is an informed decision and not a process. Living the gospel, however, does not happen

[9] TITUS 2:12

all at once, but over time as God works in us to sanctify us. It is the power of God that does this in us, and that power lies in the gospel itself, as Paul states; "For the message of the cross is foolishness to those who are perishing, but to us who are being saved it is the power of God."[10] If we do not remain in the gospel, if it is not the driving force behind our faith, we are outside of God's power and are not *being saved*.

Freedom

The gospel is the standard by which we should live. Paul told the Philippians, "Whatever happens, conduct yourselves in a manner worthy of the gospel of Christ."[11] He admonished the Colossians, "Therefore, as you received Christ Jesus the Lord, so walk in him, rooted and built up in him and established in the faith, just as you were taught, abounding in thanksgiving."[12] Though it makes a pointed command to believe and brings salvation at the moment of belief, the gospel represents a continuing relationship to God in which we are to conduct ourselves as grateful benefactors of grace. This is the standard of conduct for the one who follows Christ.

Christianity is not religious dogma. There are no hard and fast rules by which we must live. There is no legal requirement

[10] 1 CORINTHIANS 1:18
[11] PHILIPPIANS 1:27
[12] COLOSSIANS 2:6 (ESV)

that we need to meet, no works that we must do to be saved or stay saved. We need to conduct our lives knowing that we are sinners who by all rights would be condemned if Christ had not purchased our pardon with his own blood. We operate in the power of his resurrection which brought us life through the Holy Spirit. The gospel teaches us that we are free to serve God as he leads us, setting aside all else. The epistles make it clear that Paul expected this message to be the power of God in the life of a believer.

In the second chapter of Galatians, Paul speaks of a disagreement he had with Peter. Peter had been in Antioch for some time and had been eating along with the gentile believers until some other Jewish believers arrived from Judea. When they came, Peter withdrew from the gentiles out of fear of the circumcised believers.

Here is how Paul judged that Peter was in the wrong: "*When I saw that they were not acting in line with the truth of the gospel*, I said to Peter in front of them all, 'You are a Jew, yet you live like a Gentile and not like a Jew. How is it, then, that you force Gentiles to follow Jewish customs?'"[13] Peter and the other Jewish believers were 'not acting in line with the truth of the gospel'. The gospel truth is that we are free from human regulation. Anything that sets itself up to replace the gospel in

---

[13] GALATIANS 2:14

the form of rules or principals is a false gospel. Any teaching that attempts to bring us into subjection to human standards (or even the law of God) will inevitably draw us away from the power of God that brings about true holiness. "Such regulations indeed have an appearance of wisdom, with their self-imposed worship, their false humility and their harsh treatment of the body, but they lack any value in restraining sensual indulgence."[14]

One of the greatest struggles that we face as Christians is in keeping ourselves from becoming subjected to the law. The law has no power to subject us, but we can (consciously or unconsciously) choose to return to living under the law. Inevitably this will lead to a desire to return to the anonymity of darkness; disregarding the marvelous freedom we have been given. The gospel must always be in front of our eyes as a means of reminding us that we did not start our relationship with God by our own power and we cannot continue it under our own power. The minute we start thinking that we are pleasing God by what we do rather than by faith in Christ, we are in danger.

If we have entered the Kingdom of God by humble acceptance of our need for God's mercy, we must be aware that it is continued humility and absolute desperation for His mercy

[14] COLOSSIANS 2:23

that allows the power of God to work out our salvation. I, with Paul, must continually say that "I will boast all the more gladly about my weaknesses, so that Christ's power may rest on me."[15] As it was by faith that we were justified in God's sight, so it is by faith that we are to be sanctified, apart from our works.

Conclusion

When we approach Christianity as a matter of duty or a set of regulations, we can only end up frustrated. The Savior did not die to establish a new set of rules, but a way to righteousness that allows us to approach God and discover from Him His will for our lives. We can know Him, and be known, only through this incredible message of reconciliation. In power, in example, in love, Christ has established a new way of life by faith in the completed work of the cross. That is the Gospel Truth.

[15] 1CORINTHIANS 12:9

AFTERWORD

If I could summarize all of these words, it would be something like this; live and serve in humble knowledge of the righteousness of God through Christ Jesus.

When I think about everything I see around me today, particularly in the church, it breaks my heart. I have an overwhelming sense that we have come to completely ignore the power of God in our own lives and have no expectation of seeing it work in the lives of others. Leaving aside all the gifts of the Spirit (which I did not even mention) we deny the most basic truths of scriptural Christianity in our quest to create measurable results, both in our own lives and the lives of those around us.

We need to stop pretending that Christian faith is practical. It is not. The Bible paints a picture of the gospel as something completely unfathomable to humanity without the direct intervention of God. It also shows that, with God's intervention, it is the most powerful force on earth. Why we choose to ignore that power is beyond me, unless we ourselves have not experienced it which seems the only likely explanation. We can and must absolutely trust in His power alone, as clearly expressed through the gospel, to live a life pleasing to Him.

I once used this analogy in a class I was teaching; I have a hard time walking over a tall bridge because there is a part of me that wants to know what it would feel like to jump the rail and free-fall. It is the most unnerving feeling because I really don't completely trust myself not to do it and I know that it would mean certain death!

Many of us can relate this feeling to faith. There are times in our lives when we come close to God and some part of us desires to just let go of the world and completely trust Him. We won't let ourselves do it because we know beyond doubt that it will mean certain death to self. So we willfully avoid that closeness and choose to stay at a safe distance from God, seeking to preserve our lives from His infinite power to save us.

That urging that drew me to cut my bonds with the world was the Holy Spirit. One night, unable to sleep after witnessing to many at the local County fair, I began reviewing the Ten Commandments myself and came face-to-face with my sin. I suddenly recognized that I was still working to satisfy the law, and this seemed to me a sure indication that I was not saved. I met with that desperation for God's mercy that I had longed to see in others. The way to that mercy was the way of the cross.

So I jumped into the free air of the gospel truth.

I can tell you that the free-fall is breathtaking!

REFERENCES AND RESOURCES

[i] For a further exploration of this topic, I would suggest reading "Evangelism and the Sovereignty of God" by J.I. Packer, Intervarsity Press, www.ivpress.com

[ii] I strongly recommend that you listen to a teaching by Ray Comfort entitled "True and False Conversions". It is available as a free download at www.livingwaters.com.

[iii] Gordon-Conwell Theological Seminary Data, 2006

Recommended Reading

Cahill, Mark *One Thing You Can't do in Heaven*. Rockwell, TX: Biblical Discipleship Publishers, 2008   http://www.markcahill.org

Comfort, Ray & Kirk Cameron *The Way of the Master*. Alachua: Bridge-logos Publishing, 2006   http://www.livingwaters.com

Comfort, Ray *Hell's Best Kept Secret*. New Kensington: Whitaker House Publishers, 1989

About the Author

Scott Forbes is a self-employed electrical design consultant living in Neosho, Missouri. He made a 'decision for Christ' in January of 1988, but readily admits that he was never able to acknowledge the truth of the gospel until July of 2009, when he began witnessing to others after being introduced to "The Way of the Master" teachings by Ray Comfort and Kirk Cameron.

He and his wife Susan have been happily married for eleven years. He has two grown daughters, Sarah and Hannah, and a grandson, Levi, who live in California.

In addition to writing he enjoys personal evangelism, photography, bible study, music and teaching.

www.ingramcontent.com/pod-product-compliance
Lightning Source LLC
La Vergne TN
LVHW011352080426
835511LV00005B/251